DATE DUE		

938
SKE

31286111054363
Skelton, Debra.

**Empire of Alexander
the Great**

**SIMSBURY HIGH SCHOOL LMC
SIMSBURY, CT 06070**

EMPIRE OF ALEXANDER THE GREAT

REVISED EDITION

GREAT EMPIRES OF THE PAST

Empire of Alexander the Great

Empire of Ancient Egypt

Empire of Ancient Greece

Empire of Ancient Rome

Empire of the Aztecs

Empire of the Incas

Empire of the Islamic World

Empire of the Mongols

Empires of Ancient Mesopotamia

Empires of Ancient Persia

Empires of Medieval West Africa

Empires of the Maya

GREAT EMPIRES OF THE PAST

EMPIRE OF ALEXANDER THE GREAT

REVISED EDITION

DEBRA SKELTON & PAMELA DELL

JOHN W. I. LEE, HISTORICAL CONSULTANT

CHELSEA HOUSE
PUBLISHERS
An imprint of Infobase Publishing

Great Empires of the Past: Empire of Alexander the Great

Copyright © 2009 Debra Skelton & Pamela Dell

Chelsea House
An imprint of Infobase Publishing
132 West 31st Street
New York NY 10001

Library of Congress Cataloging-in-Publication Data
Skelton, Debra
 Empire of Alexander the Great / Debra Skelton & Pamela Dell. — Rev. ed.
     p. cm. — (Great empires of the past)
 Includes bibliographical references and index.
 ISBN 978-1-60413-162-8
1. Greece—History—Macedonian Expansion, 359-323 B.C. 2. Alexander, the Great, 356-323 B.C. I. Dell, Pamela. II. Title. III. Series.
 DT234.S58 2009
 938'.07—dc22   2009005723

Produced by the Shoreline Publishing Group LLC
Editorial Director: James Buckley Jr.
Series Editor: Beth Adelman
Text design by Annie O'Donnell
Cover design by Alicia Post

Printed in the United States of America

Bang MSRF 10 9 8 7 6 5 4 3 2 1

This book is printed on acid-free paper.

CONTENTS

ALEXANDER THE GREAT

J.S. Westmacott Sculp.t 1863.

INTRODUCTION

IN 336 B.C.E., A PROUD, INTELLIGENT, AND SUPREMELY ambitious young man rose to become king of Macedon, which is a kingdom on the northern border of modern-day Greece. He was only 20 years old and already wanted to take over the mighty Persian Empire to the east. He accomplished this feat and much more, despite the wealth, power, and military strength of his opponents. And he did it in just under 12 years. This illustrates his extraordinary gifts as a leader and military strategist (a person who sets strategy). It has also kept his name at the top of the list of legendary "action figures" even into the 21st century, more than 2,300 years later. He is still known throughout the world as Alexander the Great.

BORN TO GREATNESS

Alexander III of Macedon (356–323 B.C.E.) was the son of King Philip II of Macedon (382–336 B.C.E.) and Olympias of Epirus (ca. 376–316 B.C.E.) (Epirus is in what is now northwestern Greece and southern Albania), daughter of King Neoptolemus I. Alexander's birth was accompanied by various unusual events.

One of these was the burning down of the Temple of Artemis, the goddess of the wilderness, wild animals, and the hunt. Soothsayers (those who foretold the future based on signs) consulted by King Philip predicted that these events indicated his son's great destiny. Whether or not the prophecies were legitimate, the fact remains that Alexander became the most successful warrior in the history of the world.

Philip II, king of Macedon, was an aggressive leader who set a bold example for his son, Alexander.

From the age of 20 until his death at only 32, Alexander and his armies swept across a vast region that included Persia, Asia Minor, Syria, and Egypt. He traveled thousands of miles with his army. Ultimately, he ruled an empire that stretched approximately 2 million square miles over three continents. In his conquest of the world he knew he overcame armies far more powerful than his by being smarter, more resourceful, and more determined than his enemies. He also changed history by introducing Greek culture into Egypt and Asia. The spread of Greek government, language, art, and ideas laid the groundwork for civilizations that continue to this day.

After Alexander's death, his huge empire quickly fell apart, but his legendary status increased as tales of his deeds were told, passed down, and retold. His life was instructional for many other great conquerors and rulers, including Julius Caesar, Queen Cleopatra VII, and Napoleon Bonaparte.

The young prince had the best possible background for someone with great ambitions. King Philip II was an aggressive leader who set an example for his son by conquering neighboring lands when Alexander was just an infant. Alexander spent much of his childhood among the soldiers of his father's army. Philip was also a great diplomat. He married seven times, and each new marriage made a new alliance with his neighbors.

Another important influence on the young prince was his teacher Aristotle (384–322 B.C.E.), one of the greatest Greek philosophers ever to have lived. Aristotle, who wrote or edited several hundred books, taught the young prince geography, botany (the study of plants), zoology (the study of animals), logic (the study of the rules and tests of sound reasoning), and many other subjects.

CONNECTIONS

What Are Connections?

Throughout this book, and all the books in the Great Empires of the Past series, there are Connections boxes. They point out ideas, inventions, art, food, customs, and more from this empire that are still part of the world today. Nations and cultures in remote history can seem far away from the present day, but these connections demonstrate how our everyday lives have been shaped by the peoples of the past.

GREEK DISUNITY

The Greeks were renowned as statesmen, philosophers, builders, poets, dramatists, and sculptors. But Alexander grew up just as the Greeks were experiencing a period of disunity. At the time, Greece was divided into many separate city-states (a city and its surrounding farms that functions as a separate nation). Each city-state had its own army. Some of them relied on mercenaries (paid soldiers) for protection.

The main city-states, Athens and Sparta, increasingly fought among themselves for dominance. They also pulled various other city-states into alliances with them. The Peloponnesian War began between Athens and Sparta in 431 B.C.E. Eventually it involved almost all of Greece. When it finally ended in 404 B.C.E., Greece was greatly weakened.

Ancient Superheroes

Alexander and his friends did not have any comic books, television, or movies, but they did have superheroes. They read the accounts of their heroes' brave deeds primarily in the *Iliad*, a story written by the Greek poet Homer centuries before Alexander's birth. (The dates of Homer's life are not known, but he lived in the ninth or eighth century B.C.E.) Homer tells the exciting story of the Greeks' siege of Troy and the beautiful Helen, who inspired that battle, the legendary Trojan War.

The battles of great warriors and princes such as Achilles, Hector, Paris, and others, many of whom were believed to be descended directly from the Greek gods, may have inspired Alexander. In fact, the young king loved the *Iliad* so much that he memorized most of its 16,000 lines and used these super warriors as role models for his own life and values. He even slept with a copy of the *Iliad* under his pillow.

Even so, the Greeks were justifiably proud of their knowledge, language, and refinement. Their customs and ideas still had a powerful influence in the world. They thought very highly of themselves—and not so highly of their neighbors to the north, the Macedonians. In fact, although the Macedonian kings claimed that their royal family was descended from the Greek heroes Heracles and Achilles, the Greeks considered the Macedonians to be barbarians (uncivilized and uncultured) living on the fringes of Greece. But these tough frontiersmen became effective soldiers under the leadership of Philip II.

Still, 70 years after the end of the Peloponnesian War, the Greeks were no match for Macedon. Philip took advantage of their disunity by taking control of the Greek city-states one by one, through a combination of diplomacy and force. Eventually Philip's success transformed the minor kingdom of Macedon into a dominant power that ruled all of Greece. His son later surpassed this surprising military and political achievement by making Macedon, for a brief time, the most powerful kingdom in the world.

ALEXANDER IN CHARGE

When Alexander was only 16 years old, his father named him as regent, or temporary ruler, of Macedon while he was away for an extended period of time. When Thrace, one of the Macedonian allies, revolted, Alexander quickly marched troops to the area. He conquered the rebels and renamed their stronghold Alexandroupolis. It was to become the first of several cities that he named after himself.

In 338 B.C.E., at the age of 18, Alexander led the left flank (side) of the Macedonian cavalry (soldiers who fight on horseback) in the battle of Chaeronea, northwest of Athens. This decisive battle crushed the final Greek resistance to Philip's rule. Two years later in July of 336 B.C.E., Alexander became king of Macedon after Philip was murdered by one of his bodyguards. Many historians have speculated that Alexander's ambitious and ruthless mother, Queen Olympias, conspired in the plot against his father. But no factual evidence of this has been uncovered.

Philip's Greek allies, who had been forced to recognize him as their leader, saw his death—and Alexander's youth and inexperience—as an opportunity to reclaim their independence. In 335 B.C.E. Alexander turned his attention to fighting a group of tribes in the north who were rebelling against Macedon. Two of the more southern Greek city-states, Thebes and Athens, saw their opportunity and began their own uprising.

Alexander immediately swept into Greece with his troops to assert his leadership. He offered to negotiate peace with the two city-states. When Thebes refused, the young king burned down the ancient city, sparing only its temple. He killed the soldiers of Thebes and sold some 30,000 of its citizens into slavery. Athens quickly surrendered and Alexander spared that ancient city-state. Treating those who surrendered with mercy remained his usual practice for much of his life.

Alexander convinced the Greek city-states to appoint him as leader of the League of Corinth. This was a governing council his father had established a year before his death. The League members had appointed Philip to lead an invasion of the Persian Empire. They now agreed to put Alexander in charge of that invasion.

ANCIENT ENEMY

The Persian Empire was Greece's neighbor to the east. This vast empire, which stretched from Egypt and the Mediterranean Sea to India and central Asia, had dominated the ancient world for more than two centuries. It was the wealthiest and most powerful kingdom in the Middle East. Persia was also a longstanding enemy of Greece—with good reason. The Persians had started a series of wars of conquest with Greece that began in about 500 B.C.E., with the aim of expanding the Persian Empire.

In 334 B.C.E., after two years of preparation, Alexander began to put into motion the plan his father had made before his death—the

Intelligence Gathering

There is no way of knowing what Alexander dreamed of when he was a boy, because no personal records survive. But later writers often invented stories about him that claimed his desire to rule the world burned within him almost from birth. These stories eventually became widespread and were widely believed. One such story said that even as a boy Alexander may have been planning for the war with Persia. When Persian diplomats visited his father's court, the young prince questioned them at length about Persia's army, roads, communications, and customs.

invasion of the Persian Empire. He was so confident victory would be swift that Alexander set out for Persia with only enough money to pay a single month's salary to his army. He expected to meet such expenses afterwards with the riches of the Persian Empire.

Over the next three years Alexander won three major battles against the Persians. During each of these battles he was greatly outnumbered. But through quick thinking, brilliant tactics and strategy, and bravery he was able to exploit his enemy's weaknesses. In the last two of the battles, the tide started to turn against Darius III (380–330 B.C.E.), the great king of Persia, and he fled the battlefield. After the third battle some of Darius's officers murdered him. Some of these officers felt Persia could defend itself more effectively without their weak king. Some felt Alexander was certain to be victorious, and they wanted to gain his favor.

Alexander was best known as a great warrior, but he also had the makings of a strong leader. Even so, he never had a chance to rule the lands he conquered. Although many Greeks considered the Persians to be inferior barbarians, Alexander believed them to be the equals of the Macedonians and honored their customs and religions.

Everywhere Alexander and his army went they established new garrison towns (fortified towns where soldiers lived). He often appointed Persians who were friendly to him as local rulers, or allowed existing Persian rulers to remain in charge. He also explored ways to achieve harmony and equality between his soldiers and the newly conquered Persians. One way he attempted to bring this about was by organizing a mass marriage ceremony. He and about 90 of his officers married Persian women.

THE END OF THE ROAD

Alexander is considered by many to be the greatest general who ever lived. This is not only because of his military genius, but also because of his ability to inspire and motivate his men. This inspiration came from many sources. Alexander was one of the last great commanders in history to lead battles in person. Risking his safety in this way, he suffered many of the same wounds as his soldiers. He treated his soldiers exceptionally well and knew many of them personally. He also had incredible charisma—a compelling attraction that inspires others to follow.

Nevertheless, the long years away from home and the hardships the troops experienced took a toll. During the 12 years of Alexander's reign, he and his army crisscrossed the Persian Empire, traveling

20,000 miles—a distance about six times wider than the United States. They went across rugged mountain ranges, raging rivers, and scorching deserts, on foot and on horseback. They conquered everything in their path, never losing a major battle.

Finally, Alexander led his troops into India. They began conquering this country from the northeastern border of the Persian Empire. But after months of steady rain and physical hardship, the soldiers had had enough. They realized their leader was never going to willingly stop fighting and refused to continue on with him—which was their right under Macedonian law.

Alexander reluctantly headed back to Persia. It is doubtful that he intended ever to return to Macedonia. He reached Babylon (in what is now Iraq) in April 323 B.C.E., and died there about two months later, in mid-June 323 B.C.E. He was 32 years old. Rumors circulated in ancient times that he was poisoned, but modern scholars believe he died of an infectious disease, probably typhoid fever. About 13 years after Alexander's death, his wife Roxane and son Alexander IV, who was born shortly after his death, were both murdered.

In 12 years Alexander had conquered more lands and extended his leadership farther than any European ruler. He and his troops brought Greek culture, language, and ideas to these distant lands. Long after his death Greek culture continued to influence the development of many civilizations both east and west of the Tigris-Euphrates Valley.

THE MAN VS. THE LEGEND

Few figures in history have inspired more debate and controversy than Alexander the Great. Two of his generals, Ptolemy (367–283 B.C.E.) and Aristobulus (d. after 301 B.C.E.), wrote firsthand accounts of his deeds, but these were later lost. Not a single document from Alexander's time remains.

The first written history of Alexander's life to survive, *Library of History* by the Greek historian Diodorus Siculus (active 60–30 B.C.E.), was not published until nearly three centuries after his death. A second book, *History of Alexander* by Roman historian Quintus Curtius Rufus (d. 53 C.E.), was published in the first century C.E. Greek historians Arrian (ca. 86–160 B.C.E.) and Plutarch (46–ca. 122 C.E.) published biographies of Alexander in the second century C.E. Arrian wrote *The Anabasis of Alexander* and Plutarch wrote *Life of Alex-*

The Making of a Myth

Many books about Alexander were based on *The Romance of Alexander the Great*, an account that is thought to have been written in about 200 C.E. by a Greek author who came to be known as Pseudo-Callisthenes. Pseudo-Callisthenes was an unknown poet, probably of the third century, who falsely said his work was done by the scholar Callisthenes (d. 327 B.C.E.). (The real Callisthenes was the nephew of Aristotle and one of Alexander's original biographers.) Pseudo-Callisthenes' book was based on oral and written legends that were passed down after Alexander's death. The following description of Alexander's birth (as quoted in *Alexander and His Times* by Frederic Theule) shows the exaggeration that was typical of many of these early writings:

"[T]he newborn fell to the ground; there was a flash of lightning, thunder resounded, the earth trembled, and the whole world shook."

ander. *The Romance of Alexander the Great* by Pseudo-Callisthenes (dates unknown) was published in the third century.

These early histories were based on Ptolemy's and Aristobulus's accounts, as well as on stories that had been passed down verbally by people who knew Alexander or by people who had learned about him through second- or third-hand knowledge. They formed the basis for many subsequent books about the great conqueror's life.

Many of those who have told Alexander's story have been biased, slanting or exaggerating the truth sometimes for and sometimes against him. While the broader picture of his conquests and some of the facts of his background and life are confirmed, many more facts and details will never be known with any certainty.

Scholars see the great conqueror as both good and bad. Many consider Alexander an enlightened leader because he believed in the peaceful co-existence of different peoples within his empire and tried to improve the quality of life in the lands he conquered. He is considered a visionary by some. This is because he believed people should see themselves as part of a global kingdom that includes every human being, rather than as belonging just to their own nation.

Others emphasize Alexander's very real darker side. Some historians see him as a violent drunkard. They point to the facts that he destroyed some of the cities he conquered, had women and children sold into slavery, and once killed a close friend in a drunken rage. The Macedonians reportedly used brutal force to subdue some of the people they conquered. They even murdered the sick and elderly in some places. Some historians see Alexander as a self-centered tyrant who began to consider himself a god and demanded that his troops and subjects worship him. He even claimed the status of god for his horse, Bucephalas, and named a city in India after him.

Nearly all historians agree that Alexander was bisexual (he had sexual relationships with both men and women). He had a close lifelong relationship with his comrade Hephaestion, and also married several women. Homosexuality and bisexuality were accepted practices in ancient Greece and Macedon, and forming relationships with both men and women was common.

In the Middle Ages, Alexander was portrayed as a legendary hero who followed the knights' code of chivalry (the ideal of bravery and honor). In modern Iran (the center of ancient Persia) his image is that of a villain—the devil becoming a man. In trying to understand this

IN THEIR OWN WORDS

Alexander's Horse

This story of how Alexander got his famous horse, Bucephalas, was written by the Roman historian Plutarch. He is not clear what age Alexander was at the time, but historians think he was about 14 years old. Thessaly was known then for being the place where the finest horses were bred. And the price asked for Bucephalas, 13 talents, was high enough to suggest his owner thought he was an excellent animal.

There came a day when Philonicus the Thessalian brought Philip a horse named Bucephalas, which he offered to sell for 13 talents. The king and his friends went down to the plain to watch the horse's trials, and came to the conclusion that he was wild and quite unmanageable, for he . . . reared up against anyone who approached him. The king became angry at being offered such a vicious animal unbroken, and ordered it to be led away. But Alexander, who was standing close by, remarked, "What a horse they are losing, and all because they don't know how to handle him, or dare not try!"

Philip . . . asked him, "Are you finding fault with your elders because you think you know more than they do, or can manage a horse better?"

The story of how Alexander tamed his famous horse, Bucephalas, when he was just a boy became part of Alexander's legend.

"At least I could manage this one better," retorted Alexander.

"And if you cannot," said his father, "what penalty will you pay for being so impertinent?"

"I will pay the price of the horse," answered the boy. At this the whole company burst out laughing, and then as soon as the father and son had settled the terms of the bet, Alexander went quickly up to Bucephalas, took hold of his bridle, and turned him toward the sun, for he had noticed that the horse was shying at the sight of his own shadow as it fell in front of him. . . . He ran alongside the animal for a little way, calming him down by stroking him, and then, when he saw he was full of spirit and courage, he quietly threw aside his cloak and with a light spirit vaulted safely on to his back. . . .

. . . Alexander reach the end of his gallop, turn in full control, and rode back triumphant and exulting in his success. . . . [W]hen Alexander demounted [his father] kissed him and said, "My boy, you must find a kingdom big enough for your ambitions. Macedon is too small for you."

(Source: Plutarch, *The Age of Alexander: Nine Greek Lives.* Translated by Ian Scott-Kilvert. New York: Penguin Classics, 1973.)

This 1445 painting shows Alexander battling the Persians. It imagines the ancient leader wearing medieval armor. Alexander's achievements inspired kings and military leaders through the ages.

complex personality, however, it is important to keep in mind the culture of his time. Hard drinking was a common, accepted practice. So was waging war, conquering territory, and enslaving enemies.

Historians, scholars, and military experts do agree on some things. Alexander was an extremely charismatic leader with an incredibly powerful personality. They also agree that he was one of the most outstanding generals of all time. By conquering nearly the entire known world of his era, he accomplished more at a younger age and in fewer years than most people do in a lifetime.

PART · I

HISTORY

THE BEGINNING OF ALEXANDER'S EMPIRE

THE EMPIRE AT ITS LARGEST

FINAL YEARS OF THE EMPIRE

CHAPTER 1

THE BEGINNING OF ALEXANDER'S EMPIRE

WHEN ALEXANDER BECAME KING OF MACEDON IN 336 B.C.E. he inherited one of the greatest armies in the world. His father, Philip, was an extremely powerful king, and he laid the groundwork for Alexander's remarkable accomplishments. When Philip came to power in 359 B.C.E. Macedon was a poor country with many powerful noblemen who each controlled a small area. Once Philip established himself as ruler he began a systematic policy of unifying and expanding his kingdom.

During the 23 years of his rule Philip turned Macedon into a world power. He developed Macedon's mining, trade, and agriculture. He transformed a poor and backward country into a united and powerful state. He also brought Greece under Macedonian rule.

Philip established a very well-trained permanent army, making the military a full-time occupation and way of life for many Macedonian men. Before this time, soldiering had been a part-time job. Most men worked as farmers during most of the year, and were able to pick up some extra money as soldiers when they were not needed on the farm. They would then return to their farms at the start of the harvest.

Under Philip some men became soldiers year-round. This meant Philip could drill his army regularly, and much time and effort was spent on large military exercises. This built discipline and unity among the troops. Philip's military reforms and conquests helped establish this professional fighting force and created a sense of national pride among the Macedonians.

For some time Philip had been preparing for an attack on the Persian Empire. The Persians had invaded Greece 150 years earlier,

OPPOSITE

A scene from a relief carved on a sarcophagus (stone coffin) shows Alexander defeating the Persians. It was made in the late fourth century B.C.E. in Sidon, Libya.

destroying many temples and other important buildings. They still ruled several eastern Greek cities they had conquered. This neighbor was a constant threat to the Greeks. In 337 B.C.E., under Philip's influence, the Greeks agreed to declare war on their enemy to the east.

The closest part of the Persian Empire to Greece was Asia Minor (which means "lesser Asia"). It is a broad peninsula that lies between the Black Sea and the Mediterranean Sea, and corresponds roughly to what is today the country of Turkey. From there, the empire stretched to the deserts of present-day Iran in the east, to India in the southeast, and to Egypt in the southwest.

Philip was the supreme commander of the combined Greek and Macedonian forces. He sent about 10,000 soldiers to attack the coast of Asia Minor in the spring of 336 B.C.E. His plan was to join this force and lead the charge into Persia. But when he was assassinated this task fell to Alexander.

Alexander was ready to take up the throne. Philip had certainly set the stage for his son, but Alexander's successes were entirely his own. Making use of the army his father had created, he extended the power, wealth, and influence of Macedon and Greece farther than Philip probably ever dreamed possible.

VICTORY BEGINS AT HOME

Before Alexander could carry out his father's plans to attack Persia, he had to spend about two years getting control of matters at home. After Philip's death, some of the tribes from Thrace, along Macedon's northern frontier, rebelled. While Alexander was away fighting them, two of the major Greek city-states, Athens and Thebes, decided it would be a good time to shake off Macedonian rule. King Darius III of Persia made it even more tempting by offering them a bribe. They, too, rebelled.

The two city-states had underestimated the young king. Alexander quickly moved into Thebes with his army and demanded surrender. When the Thebans refused, Alexander's soldiers burned down the city and sold its citizens into slavery. This served as a warning to other Greeks who were considering rebellion. Athens quickly surrendered. Alexander accepted Athens's surrender and did not destroy the city or punish its citizens. His respect for this city-state that was the center of Greek culture continued for the rest of his life.

Alexander now prepared to carry out his father's plans to attack the Persian Empire. There were two official reasons both Alexander and his father gave for this attack. The first was to avenge the Persians' earlier destruction of Greek temples and other precious buildings. The second was to liberate the Greek cities of Asia Minor. The real purpose, however, may have been the need for money. Although Philip had greatly increased Macedon's wealth, some historians believe the kingdom was about to go bankrupt. Persia's rulers were weaker than they had ever been, so it was a good time to take control of this wealthy enemy. Alexander also wanted to win his own fame.

In the early spring of 334 B.C.E., Alexander borrowed enough money from the Macedonian treasury to keep his troops supplied for a month. Then he left Macedonia with an army of about 30,000 infantry (soldiers who fight on foot) and 5,000 cavalry. The army was made up of Macedonians, troops drawn from throughout Greece, and soldiers from the Balkan lands to the north. Alexander left some trusted generals behind, with enough soldiers to keep the peace in Macedon and Greece.

Traveling an average of 20 miles a day, Alexander and his troops reached the Hellespont in 20 days. This narrow strip of water separates Europe and Asia, in what is today Turkey. When they crossed it, they were in Persian territory.

Upon his arrival, Alexander visited the ruins of Troy. He was familiar with Homer's the *Iliad* and its legendary tales of heroes and warriors whom he believed to be his ancestors. While historians today are not sure if any of the events in the *Iliad* actually happened, in Alexander's day people regarded the tale to be a true history. In Alexander's mind, Troy was the site of the first Greek invasion of Asia, about 900 years before him. Now he came to conquer again.

At Troy, Alexander made a sacrifice at what local legend said was the grave of the Greek hero Achilles. He also dedicated his army to the Greek goddess Athena, who, in times of war, was worshipped as the goddess of intelligence and cunning. He was ready to take on the Persians.

THE BATTLE OF GRANICUS

Between 334 and 331 B.C.E., Alexander won three decisive battles against the Persian Empire. The first of these was at the Granicus River (today Koçabas Çay in Turkey) in May of 334 B.C.E. King Darius III did not take his young enemy seriously, and did not even come to the battlefield.

Instead, he sent the local satrap, or regional governor, and a force of Persian cavalry and Greek mercenaries to turn back the invaders.

The Persian troops met Alexander's forces at the river. The Persians were lined up along the steep eastern bank of the Granicus River in a strong position. They had positioned their cavalry in front and their infantry in back, which was the standard defensive formation of the Persian army. Alexander quickly saw that this formation would keep the Persian cavalry boxed in and unable to maneuver easily. The Macedonian king attacked at once, even though it was late in the afternoon. He feared that if he waited, the Persians might realize their mistake and reorganize their troops. Alexander himself led the charge directly across the Granicus. The Macedonians had to cross the deep, rapid river and climb the steep banks of the river to attack.

There was savage fighting. Alexander was injured and lay unconscious for a short time as the battle raged around him. He regained consciousness, got back on his horse, Bucephalas, and charged into the center of the Persian troops. Soon, the Macedonians had gained the upper hand. As the Persians retreated, many men were trampled by their fleeing comrades. The Macedonians killed most of the Persian soldiers they encountered. They were especially brutal toward the Greek mercenaries who fought for the Persians (they viewed those Greeks as traitors), hacking them into pieces. About 2,000 Greek mercenaries survived the battle. They were shipped back to Macedon to work in the mines as slaves.

Alexander lost only about 150 soldiers at Granicus. He buried them with military honors and promised to pay their debts back home. He also excused their families from paying taxes in the future. The victory at Granicus opened Asia Minor to Alexander and his army. As they marched south along the Aegean Sea, many cities that had previously been conquered by the Persian Empire welcomed them as liberators. He became even more popular as his generous treatment of those who surrendered became widely known.

After the battle at Granicus, Alexander saw the wisdom of capturing Persia's coastal cities before driving deeper into the country. The Persians had a powerful fleet of warships, and he did not have the naval strength to defeat them at sea. As long as the Persian fleet sailed the Mediterranean, they would remain a threat. Alexander realized that by capturing key ports that supplied the Persian ships with food and water, the navy would eventually have to surrender. He also needed to control the ports in order to ship reinforcements and supplies to his army.

Sent Home in Chains

After his victory at Granicus, Alexander laid a brutal sentence on the captured Greek mercenaries who had fought against him in that battle. They were sent, disgraced and in chains, back to Thrace, the ancient territory bounded by Macedonia on the southwest and the Danube River on the north. These unfortunate mercenaries lived out the rest of their lives doing hard labor in the silver mines there. Some of their manacled (handcuffed) skeletons have been found in Thrace by modern-day archaeologists.

The coastal city of Miletus resisted, and a Persian fleet of 400 ships with 80,000 men headed there to reinforce the city. Alexander's brilliant solution was simply to blockade the harbor so the Persian ships could not bring their troops ashore. Miletus fell quickly. But Alexander was so impressed by the courage of the Greek mercenaries who fought there that, unlike earlier battles, he accepted them into his army.

Alexander used the same technique along the east coast of the Aegean Sea. This kept the Persian fleet from being able to get fresh water and supplies. Despite its huge size, Persia's mighty navy was defeated, simply because Alexander's army managed to capture so many coastal cities. About a year and a half after Alexander's first onslaught, the entire Persian fleet disbanded.

THE BATTLE OF ISSUS

By 333 B.C.E., Alexander reached the coast of Syria. In October of that year, in a fierce battle at Issus (a coastal plain between what is now Turkey and Syria), the Macedonians had their second major encounter with the Persian army. This time, Darius was there to lead his troops into battle.

The Persians outnumbered the Macedonians, but they made a deadly mistake. They chose to fight on a narrow plain bordered by the sea, a river, and mountains. Alexander ordered his infantry to charge

This detail from a first century B.C.E. Roman mosaic shows Alexander the Great at the Battle of Issus.

A Knotty Problem

Alexander's smallest conquest has become one of his most famous. In 333 B.C.E., before the Battle of Issus, he entered the city of Gordium in what is now Turkey. In the local temple of Zeus sat a wagon that legend said belonged to King Gordius, the father of Midas. Holding the wagon's yoke (the crosspiece that holds the animals in place) to its shaft was the legendary Gordian knot. It was a complex, tightly-woven mass whose undetectable ends were buried deep within the knot itself.

An ancient prophecy said that the person who untied the Gordian knot would become the ruler of Asia. Many had attempted this task, but no one had been able to so much as loosen the knot. Alexander also tried and was unsuccessful at first. But, unlike the others, he refused to accept failure.

As usual, there is more than one story about what happened next. By one account, Alexander used his brains to solve the problem. After studying the knot, he pulled out the wooden pin that held it to the yoke to the shaft, and the knot came undone. But according to the most dramatic tales, Alexander, in typically aggressive fashion, simply slashed through it with one powerful hack of his sword. In any case, he did indeed go on to fulfill the Gordian prophecy.

Today, the term *Gordian knot* is still in modern vocabulary. It means an especially complicated and difficult problem whose solution does not seem obvious.

into a heavy shower of arrows. With his personal regiment, the Companion cavalry, he charged directly into the Persian lines and broke them up. They had no room to maneuver around the Macedonian charge.

Darius had one strategic success at Issus: He was able to maneuver some of his forces behind Alexander. But it was not enough. The Macedonians quickly overwhelmed the Persians. The Persians lost an estimated 100,000 soldiers at Issus. Only about 450 Macedonians are believed to have been killed. Darius fled, followed by many of his men. He left behind his chariot (a light, fast cart pulled by horses) and royal cloak and abandoned a fortune in gold.

He also abandoned his mother, wife, and daughters in a royal tent that was set up behind the battlefield. This tent was more luxurious than anything the Macedonians had ever seen. Alexander surprised the Persians by treating his royal captives as honored guests instead of killing them—as was the custom of the time. Over time, he even developed a very close relationship with Darius's mother, Sisygambis. That relationship continued until the end of his life.

THE SIEGE OF TYRE

Alexander now marched south through Phoenicia (a territory that now roughly comprises the coastal area of Lebanon). The major port cities of Sidon and Byblos (now Jubayl in Lebanon) surrendered to him without a fight. But when Alexander arrived at the fortified island of Tyre in February 332 B.C.E., the city refused to let him enter. Tyre was a walled fortress off the coast of what is now Lebanon. It was also a strategic coastal base, and Alexander knew he had to capture it. But gaining control of the island city would prove to be his most difficult military operation so far.

Tyre lay about a half mile off the mainland. The water surrounding it was about 18 feet deep and its walls were about 150 feet high. Its harbor was well fortified and there was no land beyond the city walls. Alexander decided to lay siege to Tyre—a military move in which the army surrounds and blocks off a city in an attempt to starve out its residents.

He hired thousands of local workers to help the Macedonian soldiers build a mole—a massive land bridge, or causeway—that reached from the mainland to the island. To build this causeway, they used debris from the old city of Tyre, which by then was an abandoned ruin on the mainland. They drove wooden piles into the seabed to support the mole and piled rocks and logs on top.

The work was extremely difficult and dangerous, and the Tyrians did not make it any easier. They used special catapults (military machines used for throwing large objects) to hurl stones and balls of burning debris at their enemies, and shot arrows at them. They captured some of the Macedonians and slaughtered them, then tossed them into the sea in view of their comrades. But Alexander's men, using screens and shields to protect themselves, continued building the mole.

When they finally finished, the mole was about half a mile long and 200 feet wide. Unfortunately for the Macedonians, the wall where the land bridge came ashore was too strong for them to batter down. But

Adopted Mother

One of Alexander's closest friendships was with Sisygambis, the mother of King Darius III of Persia. After being abandoned by her son as he fled the battlefield at Issus, Sisygambis expected death for herself, along with the Darius's wife and children. When Alexander instead treated the royal family with kindness and honor, Sisygambis gained an unexpected respect for the conqueror. A friendship was born.

Over the years, Alexander visited Sisygambis when he could and sent her many gifts. He addressed her as "mother." When Alexander died, the depth of their bond was truly revealed. Upon receiving the news of his death, Sisygambis turned her face to the wall. She remained there, refusing to eat, until she died of starvation.

Among the innovative weapons used by the Macedonian army were siege towers that could be taken apart and put back together in different shapes. According to *Library of History* by Diodorus Siculus, each floor of the 60-foot wood and metal towers ". . . had two stairways, one to bring up the material and the other one to go down, so that all the servicing was done without disorder. And 3,400 people, chosen for their strength, were in charge of moving the machine, all of them pushing at the same time, some from the interiors, others from behind and the sides," (quoted in *Alexander and His Times*, by Frederic Theule).

at the same time the mole was being built, Alexander also constructed several 150-foot portable wooden towers, or siege towers, which were covered with iron plates to make them fireproof. Battering rams (heavy objects swung or rammed against a door or wall to break it down), catapults, or siege engines—machines that throw a projectile—were then mounted on these towers.

Alexander also took over about 120 ships from the nearby city of Sidon, and put siege engines on their decks. In August 332 B.C.E., these ships moved in to attack Tyre from both north and south. The Tyrians piled rocks in the water around their island to keep the ships from coming near. They used their catapults to throw enormous boulders in hopes of sinking the ships, and they poured boiling liquids and red-hot sand on them.

The Tyrians held out for seven months against Alexander's siege, but eventually were defeated. Alexander and his men destroyed most of the city, massacred more than 8,000 Tyrians, and sold the remaining 30,000 residents into slavery. This slaughter was intended as punishment for the way the Tyrians had treated Macedonian prisoners, as well as a warning to other cities.

ONWARD TO EGYPT

After his victory at Tyre, Alexander headed for Egypt. This was the richest part of the Persian Empire. Its farms grew the best wheat and fruit in all the Mediterranean lands, and its ancient culture was widely admired.

The Egyptians hated the Persians, and welcomed Alexander as a liberator. They turned over their entire treasury to him and crowned the 24-year-old Macedonian pharaoh (king) of Egypt. Along with the title came the status of a god: The Egyptians considered Alexander (and all their pharaohs) to be the son of Ammon, their most important god.

This made a deep impression on the young king, who had always considered himself to be extraordinary. He began to wear a headdress with two rams' horns, which was a sacred symbol also worn by Ammon.

Alexander spent six months in Egypt, where he founded the great ancient city of Alexandria. Alexandria grew into a worldwide center of culture and learning, and is still a thriving and respected city today.

IN THEIR OWN WORDS

Massacre in Tyre

Alexander showed no mercy when his army finally captured Tyre. The Roman author Quintus Curtius Rufus based this account on earlier Greek sources. He describes how some people escaped, but many others were crucified on the beach. Crucifixion was a common form of execution in the ancient Mediterranean world.

> Alexander ordered all but those who had fled to the temples to be put to death and the buildings to be set on fire. . . . Young boys and girls had filled the temples, but the men all stood in the vestibules of their own homes ready to face the fury of their enemy.

> Many, however, found safety with the Sidonians among the Macedonian troops. Although these had entered the city with the conquerors, they remained aware that they were related to the Tyrians . . .

> and so they secretly gave many of them protection and took them to their boats, on which they were hidden and transported to Sidon. Fifteen thousand were rescued from a violent death by such subterfuge.

> The extent of the bloodshed can be judged from the fact that 6,000 fighting men were slaughtered within the city's fortifications. It was a sad spectacle that the furious king [Alexander] then provided for the victors: 2,000 Tyrians, who had survived the rage of the tiring Macedonians, now hung nailed to crosses all along the huge expanse of the beach.

(Source: Curtius Rufus, Quintus. *History of Alexander the Great of Macedonia*. Translated by John Yardley. "Alexander Takes Tyre." Available online. URL: http://www.livius.org/aj-al/alexander/alexander_t09.html. Accessed June 10, 2008.)

THE BATTLE OF GAUGAMELA

Alexander left Egypt in the spring of 331 B.C.E. and returned to Tyre to gather his troops. Through the spring and summer, they prepared for their next battle, at Gaugamela. This would turn out to be the decisive clash for the Persian Empire.

King Darius had been preparing for this encounter with Alexander since his humiliating defeat at Issus. He gathered a large number of soldiers and added new weapons to his army. He fitted the wheels of 200 chariots with razor-sharp, curved blades that could slash the legs of the enemy's horses and infantry. He also brought in 15 Indian war elephants.

CONNECTIONS

Alexandria, Egypt

Among the myths that persist about Alexander the Great is that he founded 57 ancient cities. Mostly, though, what he founded were military outposts. According to modern scholars, only six cities can be directly attributed to Alexander by either literary or archaeological evidence. We do know, though, that the ancient world through which Alexander passed ended up with many cities named Alexandria.

The first Alexandria, and one Alexander certainly founded himself, was in Egypt. Alexander located the city near the mouth of the Nile River, on the Mediterranean Sea. It was a perfect spot for the city to develop into a center of commerce between Egypt and the Mediterranean. He helped plan the city, and designed the streets to run in a grid pattern of straight lines.

A diverse population of Greeks, Egyptians, Persians, Syrians, and Jews soon settled in Alexandria. It remained a center of commerce, culture, and learning for the next thousand years. About 1,000 ships could use its docks at one time. Its library, built shortly after Alexander's death, was famous throughout the ancient world. It contained the world's largest collection of scrolls—about 500,000 volumes—and scholars came from all over the world to study them.

Today, Alexandria is a thriving city of about 3 million people. It is the second largest city in Egypt, and is still Egypt's chief port. Merchant ships have sailed to and from its harbors for the last 2,300 years. Historians consider the city of Alexandria to be among the most important results of Alexander's conquests.

The battle took place near the village of Gaugamela, east of the Tigris River in what is now Iraq. Darius chose the broad plain as the battle site to make sure his troops would not get hemmed in, as they had at Granicus and Issus. He had workers smooth over rough spots on the field to level the ground for his special chariots. In some spots his soldiers placed metal spikes on the ground to cripple the Macedonian horses.

Alexander reportedly had 40,000 infantry and 7,000 cavalry. Historians estimate Darius's army numbered about 100,000 soldiers.

Alexander lured the Persians into attacking his right and left flanks. This opened up a gap in their center, where Darius was fighting. Seizing the moment, Alexander quickly led his cavalry through to the center and galloped toward Darius, killing his chariot driver. Before he could get to the Persian king, however, Darius leapt from the chariot and fled the battlefield on horseback. Most of his men soon followed.

Estimates of casualties at Gaugamela vary, depending on the source. Historians have estimated the Persians lost anywhere from 40,000 to 200,000 soldiers. Macedonian losses have been estimated at 150 to 1200 soldiers.

Some historians call the Battle of Gaugamela the greatest battle of antiquity. Its outcome ended more than two centuries of Persian rule in Asia.

ALEXANDER'S ARMY

In Alexander's time, soldiers fought on foot and on horseback, meeting each other on the battlefield face to face. There were no guns, bombs, or tanks. Weapons included bows and arrows, swords, spears, chariots, javelins (light spears that are thrown), catapults, and special artillery used for sieges.

Alexander inherited from his father the best army of his day. When Philip became king of Macedon in 359 B.C.E., most Greek armies consisted of both civilians and professional soldiers (the exception was the Greek city-state of Sparta). His first innovation was to create a completely professional army. By using only professionals, warfare was no longer a seasonal activity—fought when the soldier/farmers did not have to tend their fields. Battle became possible year round.

All the helmets, shields, and weapons were made by skilled metalworkers. They beat the armor into shape from sheets of bronze. Iron was used for spearheads and swords because it is a much harder metal.

The infantry was the backbone of Alexander's army. More than twice as many soldiers made up the infantry as the cavalry. The infantry included mercenary soldiers from a variety of places. These included Agrianians (natives of modern Bulgaria), Thracians, Cretans, and Paeonians. The infantry was broken up into units according to nationality. Each unit had its own distinctive armor.

Infantry soldiers generally fought in a formation called a phalanx, which was developed by the Greeks. But Philip transformed the Greek phalanx into a devastating formation, the Macedonian phalanx. In the Greek phalanx, soldiers were arranged close together in rows. The men stood in solid ranks, forming a tight rectangle. Each soldier held a heavy shield in his left arm. Their shields covered their own left

---

Immortal Soldiers

Persia's king Darius III had a personal bodyguard of 10,000 soldiers. These specially chosen soldiers were called The Immortals, because when a soldier was killed, a new recruit immediately replaced him.

This Macedonian body armor is made of iron and decorated with gold. The piece dates from about 350 B.C.E. and was found in a tomb in Verginia, Greece. It was once thought to be King Philip II's tomb, but historians now think the tomb was built for Alexander's half-brother, who was also named Philip.

shoulders and overlapped each other, so that each soldier's shield also protected the man to his left. But because their left arm was supporting a heavy shield, the Greek soldiers could only use a relatively short spear in the right hand.

Philip replaced the large shield with a smaller one slung over the left shoulder. This freed up both hands. It enabled the soldiers in the Macedonian phalanx to carry a long pike, called a *sarissa*, in both hands. The *sarissa* was made of wood and had an iron tip. It was so long—estimates are from about 16 feet to as much as 24 feet—that even those carried by men in the back rows stuck out beyond the front row of men.

From the front, a Macedonian phalanx resembled a giant porcupine or hedgehog. It was 16 rows deep. The *sarissas* of the first five rows pointed forward, producing an impenetrable forest of armor-piercing iron. The other rows of soldiers held their *sarissas* at an upward angle, forming an effective protection against objects hurled at them.

A phalanx could move in a straight, angled, or curved line, or swing around as a solid mass to face the opposite direction. If the *sarissas* were held horizontally and thrust forward during a charge, they sliced through the enemy. Since the pikes were so long, opposing armies had difficulty getting close enough to attack the members of the phalanx. This was a great advantage.

Additionally, when these awesome weapons were held upright together, they created a wall of spears. This hid from the enemy's view any maneuvers going on behind the phalanx. This was a great aid to surprise moves. Seeing the deadly wall of a phalanx's spears coming toward them must have had a terrifying effect on Alexander's enemies.

The phalanx and the cavalry trained together to coordinate their actions. The phalanxes were generally used to hold the enemy's army in one place so the cavalry could smash them. The Companion cavalry was an elite body of noble Macedonians led in battle by Alexander himself. He adopted this innovation from his father. Such a highly disciplined cavalry could force an enemy's flank to turn, cut off its retreat, or pursue fleeing soldiers.

Alexander's cavalry squadrons were divided into smaller units called platoons. Their commanders were chosen based on personal merit, rather than race or birth. Cavalry soldiers were armed with *sarissas* and outfitted with open-faced iron helmets and short body armor that protected their chests and backs.

The cavalry used disciplined, dense formations, such as wedges and diamonds. The officer at the tip of the formation would find weak points in the enemy's line and then order a charge. Even though they had no stirrups or saddles (they had not yet been invented), the cavalry charged at a gallop. They were trained to respond immediately to commands on the field of battle. They could drive home a charge and then immediately reform, ready for another order.

The Macedonian cavalry was the most effective cavalry in the ancient world. Working together with such a sophisticated and

CONNECTIONS

Alexander's Weapons

Catapult: The Greeks invented catapults in about 400 B.C.E. Philip was the first commander to use them on the battlefield, and Alexander adopted the same practice. During the Roman Empire, catapults had a long arm that was used like a lever to fling enormous boulders. But Alexander's soldiers used smaller, more mobile catapults to fire large arrows and stones, or bags of stones, capable of killing or wounding a number of men with a single shot.

Rather than a lever, these smaller catapults were more like giant crossbows. They were generally designed on a horizontal plane with arms of wood. Human hair or animal sinew was wrapped around each arm and acted like a spring to send the arrows or stones hurtling forward. They were extremely accurate in hitting intended targets but had the disadvantage of not being able to travel very far.

These smaller catapults are called *ballistae*. The Greek word comes from another Greek word, *ballei*, meaning "to throw." These words are also the ancient roots of our modern word *ballistics,* the science of the way projectiles move in flight, or more specifically, the study of what happens when firearms are fired. Most people today have heard of ballistic missiles. These are one of the more destructive modern equivalents of ancient projectile weaponry.

Battering Ram: The battering rams used by ancient armies were most often made of the largest tree trunk possible. Then they hacked it to a point at one end. The tree trunk would be set on wheels, or sometimes carried by men, and rammed through the doors and walls of fortresses and castles. Sometimes a battering ram was slung in a support frame so that it could be repeatedly swung against the barricade.

Modern battering rams are usually used by police forces, most often by special paramilitary units known as SWAT (special weapons and tactics) teams, which are specially trained for dangerous missions. Sometimes these battering rams are attached to cars or other heavy vehicles and sometimes they are smaller, used by just two or three officers to break down a door.

terrifying method of attack as the phalanx, they changed the nature of warfare. Alexander went on to develop his father's methods further, using them to great advantage across two continents. His tactics were later adopted by other leaders.

Alexander's use of huge siege machines at Tyre introduced a new age of warfare. Between 332 and 326 B.C.E., Alexander mounted 15 sieges. His mechanics and engineers developed special weapons for sieges, including battering rams, catapults, and mobile towers.

The catapults could hurl 20- or 30-pound stone blocks as far as 500 feet onto a battlefield or over a wall. They were also used to hurl large arrows and possibly even poisonous snakes and hornet nests. Alexander's catapults were similar to huge crossbows—a type of giant bow and arrow. These stable weapons also shot arrows that were up to three feet long. Soldiers would often set fire to the giant arrows before launching them.

Although the Macedonian army was a much stronger fighting force than its navy, Alexander used many different kinds of ships in his campaigns. The most famous were *triremes* from Athens—Greek battleships that had 170 oarsmen arrayed in three tiers. The ships weighed up to 2,200 pounds but were fast and easy to maneuver. The oarsmen rowed in unison at a speed of up to 18 beats per minute. The beat of a gong or a drum was used to maintain this rhythm.

The main weapon of the *trireme* was a battering ram that stuck out from the bow at the water level. It was made of oak and reinforced with a bronze cap. The rowers propelled the *trireme* against an enemy hull. The ram pierced the hull, then the oarsmen rowed backwards to free their *trireme* from the sinking ship.

The navy sailed on seas, rivers, and small bodies of water. Because the *triremes* carried so many men, there was not a lot of room onboard for provisions. This meant that typically they could not stay at sea for long stretches of time. So the *triremes* traveled from one island to the next or stopped frequently along the shore. They almost always beached for the night.

HOW ALEXANDER BEAT DARIUS

Alexander was greatly outmatched by Darius in almost every way. The Persians had many more troops and ships and greater wealth. With a force of Greek mercenaries estimated at up to 50,000, the Persians may have even had more Greek soldiers fighting on their side than Alexander had on his.

Even the size of the two men made them unequal. Darius, then in his mid-40s, was said to have been nearly six and a half feet tall—huge for the time. Alexander was in his 20s and of medium height.

Tactics and Strategy

Warfare involves both tactics and strategy. Tactics are the techniques and procedures used by soldiers in the heat of battle. Strategy is the overall battle plan, worked out in advance. Alexander came up with brilliant strategies that were later adopted by other generals, such as Napoleon. But a good strategy only works if the enemy does exactly what they are expected to do. Since this rarely happens, it is equally important for a great general to be good at tactics—the art of maneuvering forces in combat. Alexander is also considered one of the greatest tacticians in military history. These two gifts are rarely combined in one military leader.

Yet Alexander had a number of advantages that enabled him to overcome his enemy's strength and size. His men were veterans who had fought with his father and were used to working together. They were extremely disciplined and committed, even devoted, to their leader.

The Persian forces were not as well trained, well disciplined, or devoted. They did not have a lot of experience fighting together. They came from many places in the vast Persian Empire, and they did not have a common language, equipment, or command structure. Their size even worked against them at times because they were not as fast or flexible as Alexander's army.

Alexander was an expert at analyzing what his available men and weapons could do, at coordinating his troops for complex battle maneuvers, and at hiding their real numbers. He was able to seize opportunities that opened up during a battle and organize his troops on the spot to make the most of their abilities and to exploit his enemy's weaknesses and mistakes.

One of the young king's greatest advantages was his bravery. A courageous and even reckless leader, he always led his troops into battle. His helmet was made of polished iron and shined so that everyone could see him on the battlefield. Two long white feathers rose from it, to make sure that even at great distances his men could see that he was fighting along with them.

Alexander inspired a rare depth of loyalty in his men. This was partly due to the stirring speeches he gave before battles. He also treated his soldiers very well and knew a great number of them by name. He also had tremendous charisma, or personal magnetism and charm. (The English form of this word is based on the Greek word *kharis*, which means "outward grace or favor.") Many of Alexander's men believed that the gods favored their ruler and his cause. Because

The Egyptians considered Alexander to be the son of the god Ammon. So he began to wear a headdress with ram's horns, a sacred symbol of Ammon. This silver coin showing Alexander's image with horns (ca. 305–281 B.C.E.) comes from Thrace.

of this, they were willing to follow him into battles and fight bravely, even when they were outnumbered.

Another factor is that the Persians underestimated Alexander, especially in the beginning. Memnon (380–333 B.C.E.), the general who led those Greek mercenaries fighting for the Persians, came up with an excellent plan even before the battle of Granicus. Memnon suggested that instead of fighting the Macedonians, the Persians starve them out by burning Persian cities and destroying the crops in their path. He knew that the Macedonian army, no matter how fierce, would not be able to survive for long without food and supplies.

Most likely, this plan would have defeated Alexander. But Memnon died of disease before he could put it into effect. Darius's commanders chose to engage Alexander. It was a decision they came to regret.

CHAPTER 2

THE EMPIRE AT ITS LARGEST

ALEXANDER'S VICTORY AT GAUGAMELA ESTABLISHED HIM as the ruler of the Persian Empire. Only three years after he first invaded Asia Minor he was hailed as the new Great King of Persia and Lord of Asia—the ruler of all Persian lands.

But as long as Darius III was alive he remained a threat to Alexander's rule. As soon as Alexander was able to break away from the fighting at Gaugamela he began his pursuit of Darius. Alexander pursued the older king through the night, but Darius escaped into the mountains. Alexander decided to wait rather than to push through dangerous mountain passes, where troops still loyal to Darius could ambush the Macedonians.

Darius had abandoned some of his treasure near Gaugamela, and Alexander used the loot to reward his soldiers. He then traveled south along the centuries-old Royal Road to Babylon (located near what is now Baghdad). He expected opposition, but instead, because the Persian king was unpopular, the Babylonians welcomed the soldiers with trumpets and showered them with flowers. The young king's popularity grew when he promised to rebuild the temple to the chief Babylonian god, Bel Marduk, which the Persians had destroyed.

The Macedonians and Greeks were amazed by the wealth and majesty of Babylon. This fabled city already had a history dating back to about 2000 B.C.E. It was nearly five times larger than Athens, and was organized around a seven-story tower—which may have been the famous Tower of Babel mentioned in the Bible.

The Macedonian troops remained in Babylon for five weeks. Alexander took up residence in one of Babylon's two royal palaces. The

OPPOSITE

Not much remains of the great palace at Persepolis (in modern Iran) after the Macedonians set it on fire in 330 B.C.E.

palace had about 600 rooms. Its terraces of trees, flowers, and shrubs, called the Hanging Gardens, were famous throughout the known world. Among the Persian treasures was a large quantity of bullion (bars of silver and gold). Alexander is said to have used some of it to give the soldiers nearly a whole year's extra pay.

Alexander began a practice of appointing local Persian officials to leading positions. In Babylon he allowed the local satrap to keep his position. Although his soldiers resented this, it was a wise policy. It meant that rebellions would be less likely, and other Persian satraps would be more willing to surrender if they knew they were likely to keep their jobs. Alexander also separated the civil government from the military. He left a military force under Macedonian command in Babylon and pushed farther east.

SUSA AND PERSEPOLIS

In November 331 B.C.E., Alexander set out for the administrative center of the Persian Empire, Susa (a spot that today is about 30 miles from the city of Shustar in Iran). On the way he encountered about 15,000 reinforcements from Greece whom he had sent for nearly a year before. Their arrival increased his military strength significantly. When the troops arrived in Susa in December, the city surrendered and turned over its treasury.

Alexander's soldiers were once again astonished by the wealth of the Persians. They discovered more gold and silver, much of it looted from Greece by the Persians more than 100 years before. They also found furnishings, tapestries, and jewels. There were piles of purple embroidery that had remained fresh for nearly 200 years because of the honey and olive oil that had been mixed into their dyes.

Alexander handed out more gifts to his men and sent a small part of the Susa treasure to Athens. That small portion, however, was equal to six times Athens's yearly income at the time.

Susa was the home of Darius's mother, Sisygambis, his daughters, and members of his harem (a group of women, usually relatives including multiple wives). All of them had been traveling under the protection of Alexander's army since they were captured at Issus. Now Alexander let them return to their palace at Susa.

While he was in the city, Alexander also reorganized his army. He was getting ready for warfare in the wilder, more mountainous country

where they would hunt for Darius. He divided the troops into smaller units of 75 to 100 men and appointed many new officers. Up until that time, the Macedonian military units were organized according to the provinces of their kingdom. For the first time, Alexander selected officers based on merit—an indication that he wanted to do away with regional divisions. The army also changed its method of sending signals. They had used bugle calls, but now they adopted the Persian method of using a large fire to send smoke signals.

Alexander appointed the Persian commander of Susa's fort as satrap of the region. In December 331 B.C.E., he and his troops once again took to the road. As usual they left soldiers behind, led by a Macedonian.

With a refreshed army of an estimated 60,000 men, Alexander marched toward the city of Persepolis. It was the ceremonial center of the Persian Empire and the winter home of the Persian kings. On the way the army met resistance in a narrow mountain pass known as the Persian Gates. The challengers were probably the last holdouts of Darius's army. Alexander divided his army into two branches to get through.

When they arrived in Persepolis, the Macedonians found the largest treasure of all. The vast storehouse of gold and silver was said to be the largest single fortune in the world. The treasure was so enormous that it took more than 500 camels and more than 4,000 mules to transport it back to Macedon. The treasure weighed around 7,300 tons, and was enough for Alexander to pay his army for 25 years.

NIGHT OF DESTRUCTION

On April 25, 330 B.C.E., after a long night of drinking, the Macedonians burned down the great palace in Persepolis. This event has remained controversial, with different historians offering different interpreta-

Persepolis

In the language of the Persians, the name of their magnificent city was Takht-e-Jamshid. It means "the throne of Jamshid." The name honored a mythical Persian king. In the West, it is known by its Greek name, Persepolis. From about 500 B.C.E., the capital city of the Persian Empire was called Persa. Add *Persa* to the Greek word for city, *polis*, and it is easy to see how the Greeks derived their version of the name—Persepolis, or City of Persians.

Technically speaking, Persepolis was not really a city at all. It was a series of palaces and treasuries that formed a ceremonial center. A small town of guards and caretakers looked after everything.

Each year at the Persian New Year's festival, diplomats from all the nations that were under Persian rule arrived at Persepolis to renew their loyalty to the king. They brought expensive gifts. The treasures were deposited at Persepolis, where they accumulated over many decades.

Although Alexander destroyed the great palace complex of Persepolis, it has not been entirely lost. Since the early 20th century, archaeologists have uncovered many of its huge structures. One of the most stunning

Modern archaeologists have uncovered many of the huge structures of the palace at Persepolis, including the *apadana*, or reception hall. These pillars decorated with carved horse heads mark the location of the *apadana*.

of these is the palace's *apadana*, or reception hall. This is where the great Persian kings received treasure from subjects who came from far and wide.

Today, the *apadana* is marked only by a wide field of pillars decorated with elaborately carved horse heads. It is a strange site, standing in the middle of a bare red desert in southwest Iran. UNESCO declared the city of Persepolis a World Heritage Site in 1979.

tions. Many have criticized the act as barbaric and unnecessary since the Macedonians controlled the city. Other historians believe that destroying the palace was an act of revenge.

The magnificent structure was built by King Darius I (d. ca. 485 B.C.E.) in about 520 B.C.E. Later it became the residence of King Xerxes I (519–465 B.C.E.), who had destroyed many Greek temples when he invaded Greece in 480 B.C.E. Still other historians claim that Persepolis was a symbol of the rule of Darius III. They suggest that destroying it was a dramatic way for Alexander to demonstrate the end of the Persian Empire.

Burning the palace was probably not an easy decision. On one hand, as a Macedonian Alexander identified deeply with Greek culture. He had come to Persia partly to avenge the wrongs Persia had committed against Greece. But he was also beginning to enjoy his role as Persia's ruler. He admired and appreciated many things about this ancient civilization. He wanted to be accepted by the Persian ruling class. He began to adopt Persian ways and brought Persian attendants into his inner circles. When they were forced to share power with the Persians some of the Macedonian soldiers began to feel discontented.

While in Persepolis, Alexander discovered that Darius had fled to his summer palace in Ecbatana (now the city of Hamadân in modern Iran). He was traveling with what was left of his army, whose numbers had been greatly reduced because so many soldiers had deserted or been killed. The remaining troops numbered only about 9,000 men, including Greek mercenaries. In the spring of 329 B.C.E., Alexander and some of his troops pushed north through the mountains toward the Caspian Sea in pursuit of Darius.

DARIUS IS BETRAYED

Hearing a report of Alexander's approach, Darius and his men began riding east. Several of Darius's own officers believed he was too weak a leader to be left in control. They took the Persian king prisoner and threw him into a wagon. Alexander set out after them with about 500 men, leaving his second-in-command, Parmenion (400–330 B.C.E.), in charge at Ecbatana. They traveled across the desert, covering more than 440 miles in just 11 days.

After the long, exhausting chase, they came upon Darius's camp at dawn. But Alexander did not get the chance to take his revenge. Bessus

(d. 329 B.C.E.), the leader of the revolt against Darius and the satrap of a region called Bactria, stabbed Darius to death just before Alexander arrived. Alexander covered Darius's body with his cloak. He sent his former enemy's body back to Persepolis, ordering that a royal funeral be held.

One of Bessus's accomplices, Nabarzanes (dates unknown), surrendered to Alexander and was pardoned. Alexander also released those mercenaries who had joined the Persians before Greece and Macedon invaded Persia. The others were required to serve in Alexander's army for the same pay that Darius had given them. Obviously Alexander's view of mercenaries had changed since the Battle of Granicus, when Greek soldiers fighting for the Persians had been murdered or enslaved as traitors.

Alexander then turned his attention to a new target: Bessus. The satrap had declared himself king after Darius. Now he was fleeing to his home region of Bactria, in what is now Afghanistan. Alexander spent much of the next year hunting him.

Bactria was at the eastern edge of a wilderness of vast deserts and rugged mountains. After their conquests of the three royal cities, Alexander and his men headed east into this dry, difficult region. It was populated by fierce nomadic tribes—people who move from place to place with no permanent settlements. To conquer the east, they would have to do battle with this new kind of opponent—and with the elements as well. Thirst, hunger, heat, and cold were to become the soldiers' new enemies during the long marches ahead.

MURDER PLOT

In October 330 B.C.E., Alexander was told about a plot against his life. The accused man, Philotas (d. 330 B.C.E.), was a lifelong friend of Alexander's and the commander of the Companion cavalry. He was also the son of Alexander's second-in-command, Parmenion.

Philotas himself was not the plotter. But he was said to have heard about a conspiracy against Alexander and failed to report it. There is no good evidence that Philotas was actually plotting anything. Still the Macedonian army found him guilty of treason. He and several others were executed.

Alexander then sent soldiers to Ecbatana where Parmenion was stationed. He was executed as well. It is unclear whether he was guilty of anything. But even if he was innocent, the tradition of the Macedonian blood-feud would have required the soldiers to kill him. Otherwise he might have felt bound to avenge his son's death. The deaths of Philotas and Parmenion added to the poor morale among the troops, which had begun with Alexander's appointment of Persians to high positions.

Many of the men felt the war was over and wanted to go home, rather than pursue Bessus in the east. But Alexander was determined to conquer the eastern half of the empire. He knew that Bessus was a bold, skillful warrior who was popular enough to organize a resistance. Moreover, Bessus was well-acquainted with the remote hills and the tribes who lived in them, so he would be fighting in familiar territory. Alexander, driven by his desire to conquer, felt compelled to stop him.

But Alexander's personal drive and courage were not enough. He needed his army behind him. Now they stood at

Alexander the Invincible

During his Asian campaigns Alexander was injured at least 10 times. He was wounded by nearly every kind of weapon, including swords, clubs, daggers, stones, and arrows. In the battle against the Mallians, an arrow pierced Alexander's lung and his troops thought he had been killed. They were so enraged that they ran through the city killing everyone they could find. Alexander made it through with a splintered rib and a torn lung.

During the siege of Gaza he was badly wounded in the shoulder and lost a great deal of blood when he was hit by a catapult bolt.

While invading Samarkand an arrow split a bone in his leg, making it impossible for him to ride his horse. At first, the infantry got the honor of carrying Alexander. But soon the cavalry became jealous of their privilege and demanded to dismount so they could carry him. Alexander decided to let each unit take turns sharing the honor.

Alexander also lived through various other minor and serious wounds and illnesses. These ranged from a bird dropping a stone on his head to getting a mild case of hypothermia while crossing the Cydnus (now called the Tarsus) River.

the threshold of a mutiny (when soldiers rebel against their commander). In a rousing speech, he offered lavish gifts to any soldiers who continued on with him. He heightened his troops' motivation by declaring that they stood on the threshold of victory. He assured them that Bessus was nothing more than a barbarian chieftain and would be easy to defeat. There was no mutiny.

DEATH MARCHES

As Alexander and his troops pursued Bessus into Bactria the young king found himself confronted with an extremely important strategic decision. The most direct way to Bactria was a route through the Kara Kum Desert. This was part of the long trade route that later came to be known as the Silk Road. The other road detoured south through several towns and then across the Hindu Kush, one of the major mountain ranges in central Asia. (Today, the Hindu Kush mountains separate Kabul in Afghanistan from central Asia.)

The direct route was easier and shorter, but it exposed Alexander and his men to attack from Bessus's dangerous archers (soldiers who shoot with bows and arrows) mounted on horseback. Alexander chose the southern detour route, taking a wide loop before heading north again up into what is now Kabul and Begram. In late May of 329 B.C.E., he marched with his troops into the Hindu Kush mountains. His teacher, Aristotle, believed that from their summit one would be able to see the end of the world.

Struggling through the same snows on the same mountain passes, modern travelers retrace the route taken by Alexander through the Hindu Kush.

Crossing the Hindu Kush is considered by many historians to be one of the most incredible accomplishments of Alexander's career. It required extreme levels of endurance and extraordinary leadership. The highest peak of the Hindu Kush is more than 25,000 feet above sea level, making it one of the highest mountains in the world. The army crossed over the 12,000-foot Khawak Pass. They were forced to travel in a single line along narrow paths. This stretched the troops out over miles.

Many of the men got altitude sickness. The intense glare caused snow blindness. There was a shortage of provisions, and nothing grew in the area except herbs. Supplies could not be moved by wagon, and the mules that carried them frequently fell on the dangerous, snow-covered roads. The men ate the dead mules raw because there was no cooking fuel. Men died of cold, hunger, and thirst.

Alexander may have lost more than 2,000 men in the march across the Hindu Kush. He arrived in Bactria with fewer than 32,000 soldiers. He released the older and sick ones from service. Then he and set off with the remaining troops, chasing Bessus toward the Oxus River.

Down out of the mountains, the soldiers faced another ordeal: heat. It was too hot to travel during the day, so they had to march at night across 46.6 miles of waterless desert. The shifting sands made travel especially difficult. The men used up all their water. A famous story about this march is that when one of the men found a small pool of water, he offered it first to Alexander. The king refused, saying that he would drink only when all his soldiers had water. It was this kind of behavior that inspired such fierce loyalty.

When the army finally reached the river, many soldiers, including Alexander, drank too much water and became ill. Some of them died.

Meanwhile, Bessus fled through Bactria. His troops from Bactria and Sogdiana were in familiar territory. (The satrapies of Bactria and Sogdiana were located in more or less the same areas as modern Afghanistan, Uzbekistan, and western Tajikistan.) They burned the plains behind them as they fled, so that their pursuers would find no food. After they crossed the Oxus River, they burned all the available ships to prevent Alexander's men from crossing the river. The Macedonians, however, made rafts by stuffing animal skins and tents with hay. Five days later Alexander's army reached the opposite bank.

Crossing the Hindu Kush, the desert, and the Oxus River made Alexander's army seem unstoppable. Bessus's allies were no longer certain they wanted to back him. In June of 329 B.C.E., about a year after Alexander

IN THEIR OWN WORDS

Deadly Desert

In the spring of 329 B.C.E, Alexander crossed the large desert between the Hindu Kush and the Oxus River, in pursuit of the Persian leader Bessus. The best description of the terrible crossing was written by Roman author Quintus Curtius Rufus, who based his account on older Greek sources.

The lack of water . . . is such that desperation produces a parching thirst even before a natural craving to drink appears. For 75 kilometers no trace of water is to be found. The heat of the summer sun scorches the sands and, when these start to heat up, everything on them is baked as if by perpetual fire. Then a misty vapor thrown up by the burning heat of the earth obscures the daylight, giving the plains the appearance of one vast, deep ocean. Travel by night seemed bearable because dew and the early morning freshness would bring relief to their bodies; but with the dawn comes the heat, draining with its aridity all natural moisture and deeply burning the mouth and the stomach.

So it was their resolution that failed first, and then their bodies. They were unwilling to stop and unwilling to go on. A few had followed the advice of people who knew the country and stored up some water. This slaked their thirst for a short time, but then the increasing heat rekindled their craving for water. Consequently, all the wine and oil in anyone's possession was consumed, too, and such was the pleasure they gained from drinking it that they had no fear of thirst in the future. Subsequently, the liquid they had greedily drained put such a weight on their stomachs that they could neither hold up their weapons nor continue their journey, and the men who had been without water now seemed to be more fortunate than they themselves, since they were forced to spew up the water they had immoderately consumed.

(Source: Curtius Rufus, Quintus. *History of Alexander the Great of Macedonia*. Translated by John Yardley. "Alexander in the Bactrian Desert." Available online. URL: http://www.livius.org/aj-al/alexander/alexander_t17.html. Accessed June 10, 2008.)

began chasing Bessus, the Sogdian leader, Spitamenes, arrested his former ally. Bessus was brought naked and tied up to the town of Bactra. Alexander turned him over to the Persian people, who put him on trial for killing their king. He was found guilty and executed.

GUERRILLA WARFARE

Since they had left the three royal Persian cities, Alexander and his men had been fighting a different kind of war. The mountainous region to the east was made up of independent, fierce tribes and bandits. These people were unknown to the Greeks, and even the Persians had only barely managed to dominate them. The Persian kings had to pay a kind of tax before the tribes would allow them to pass through their lands.

The Sogdians and the other tribes who joined forces with them to fight Alexander were excellent archers. Instead of big battles fought by armies facing one another on a battlefield, this new phase of the campaign involved guerrilla warfare. The Bactrians and the Sogdians, who lived in what is now Turkestan, did not fight in the traditional Greek-Macedonian style. Much of the landscape was dusty steppe country—semi-arid grass-covered plains—that was unsuited for phalanx maneuvers.

In response Alexander reorganized his cavalry. He developed new formations that were better suited for the new landscape. He also brought native horsemen into the army. Alexander's ability to successfully adapt his strategy and tactics to many different kinds of warfare, including major battles, sieges, skirmishes, and guerrilla opposition, sets him apart from other great commanders who were skilled primarily in conventional, open warfare.

The Macedonian army marched from its base in Maracanda, near modern-day Samarkand, to the Jaxartes River. They considered this the end of Asia. In July 329 B.C.E., Alexander founded a new city on the northeast border of the Persian Empire (the modern city of Khodzent in Tajikistan). He called it Alexandria Eschate, which means "the farthest Alexandria."

Messengers arrived, telling the Macedonians that the tribes of Sogdiana had risen up in revolt against Alexander. Their leader was a warlord named Spitamenes (370–328 B.C.E.)—the same man who had turned Bessus over to Alexander.

Spitamenes may have been the one enemy Alexander underestimated. Although his army was smaller than Alexander's, Spitamenes was probably the most determined opponent the young leader encountered. It would take Alexander until the autumn of 328 B.C.E.—more than a year—to defeat him.

Alexander spent the winter in Bactria waiting for reinforcements. His situation was dangerous. Since crossing the Hindu Kush, his army had dwindled to about 30,000 men. In the last months of 329 B.C.E., it was at its smallest. A total of 12,000 more infantry with 2,000 cavalry eventually arrived. But the reinforcements were mostly Greek mercenaries, not Macedonians.

These forces managed to capture seven Sogdian forts. During this campaign, Spitamenes' horsemen laid siege to the Macedonian garrison at Maracanda. When the Macedonians started to march south, the Sogdian tribes attacked their rear. Alexander returned to the north and sent his Greek mercenaries to Maracanda. This turned out to be one of his few serious mistakes.

Spitamenes killed most of the mercenaries. Alexander and some members of his cavalry raced to Maracanda. They traveled 180 miles through desert country in three days. But Spitamenes had escaped. The local population who had rebelled suffered the same fate the Tyrians had suffered: The men were killed and the women was sold as slaves.

Another of the local tribes to rebel in 328 B.C.E. were the Scythians. They were an extremely fierce people. Alexander was wounded in the neck during the battle to subdue them. But he continued to lead his forces. They used catapults on the battlefield to defeat the Scythians. It was a turning point in the region, because many tribes were convinced that if the Scythians could not defeat Alexander, no one could. They surrendered.

Spitamenes finally came to his end in December 328 B.C.E. Deserted by his allies, he was killed by a Macedonian officer. He himself had killed about 2,000 Macedonian infantry and 300 cavalry soldiers in Sogdiana.

CAPTURING THE SOGDIAN ROCK

In the spring of 327 B.C.E., Alexander captured one of the most secure strongholds in Asia, the Sogdian Rock. This was a short distance south of Maracanda. Sheer, steep cliffs protected the Sogdians, who occupied an area near the top. Their stronghold was full of caves that could hold a small army. They had enough provisions to last for years. Their leader, Oxyartes (b. 377 B.C.E.), taunted Alexander. He dared Alexander to send up men with wings to capture the fortress.

Alexander marched his men to the base of the rock, but there was clearly no way to climb up the face of it. A single goat track led up to the Sogdian camp, but this was defended by the expert Sogdian archers. The Macedonian army camped beyond the range of their arrows.

If Alexander did not conquer the Sogdians, their continued presence would always be a threat to his rule. He assembled 300 of his best

Rage and Murder

In Sogdiana, just before the death of Spitamenes, Alexander lost his temper in a drunken quarrel and killed a close friend, Cleitus the Black (d. 328 B.C.E.). Cleitus was the brother of Alexander's childhood nurse and one of the two commanders of the Companion cavalry. He had fought under Philip and had known Alexander his entire life. He had even saved Alexander's life at the Battle of Granicus.

There was a banquet just before Cleitus was to leave for Bactria, where he had been appointed governor. It was the Macedonian feast day for Dionysus, the god of wine. As was usual with Alexander and his court, everyone was drinking heavily. Cleitus became annoyed with Alexander's drunken boasting and made some critical remarks. Among other complaints, he was offended by the fact that the Macedonians now had to ask Persian attendants for permission to see their king. He also objected to Persians getting positions of command.

His complaints enraged Alexander. Several officers had to physically restrain their king from attacking Cleitus. There are various accounts of what happened next, but in at least one account Cleitus was quickly led out. However he was soon back with a final insult. According to the story, Alexander grabbed a spear in a rage and murdered Cleitus with a single thrust. All stories agree that Cleitus fell dead and Alexander was left covered in his blood. The king was immediately overcome by remorse, reports say, and he attempted to use the same spear to kill himself. But officers and friends prevented him from doing so.

In the following days, Alexander was filled with grief over his friend's death, and furious with himself about his lack of self-control. He became depressed, isolated himself in his tent, and refused all food, drink, or comfort.

When soothsayers accompanying Alexander gave the troops justifications for the king's violent action, Alexander finally reappeared. They claimed that the god Dionysus had possessed the king with madness to punish him for an insult on his feast day. When he recovered, Alexander made a sacrifice to Dionysus.

To take Cleitus's place, Alexander appointed a Persian officer named Artabazus (389–325 B.C.E.) as satrap of Bactria. He had known Artabazus in Macedonia, where the Persian spent many years in Philip's court during Alexander's childhood. Artabazus spoke both Greek and Persian, and became one of Alexander's most influential Persian advisors. He suppressed an uprising in Persia and helped convince the Persian elite to accept Alexander.

mountaineers and offered them lavish rewards if they successfully reached the top. In the first truly dangerous mission not that was led by Alexander himself, the men began their climb.

From his home base in Macedonia to the west, Alexander and his army stormed through what is now Turkey, south into Egypt, and east toward India. The arrow shows the path of his travels.

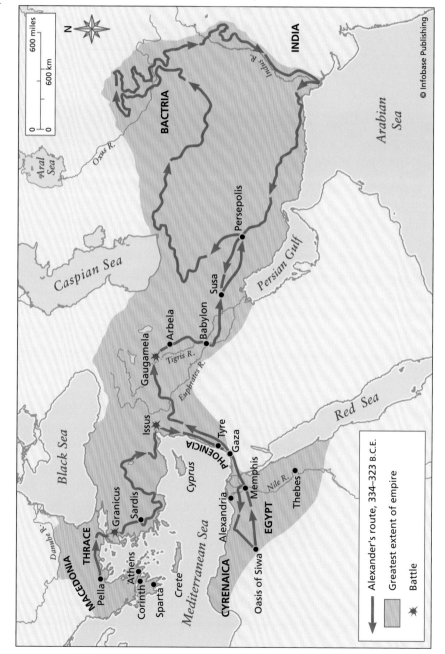

They chose to climb up the steepest side of the rock so they would not be seen by the people in the caves. About 30 of the climbers—one in 10—fell to their deaths. When the remaining men reached the top they waved the long strips of linen they had brought with them to signal their success.

The mountaineers were unarmed because they had not been able to carry their heavy arms up on the dangerous climb. Oxyartes, however, was unaware of this. He saw only that some of Alexander's men had succeeded in reaching the top of the rock. He had no idea how many nor what weapons they had, and he surrendered.

Ultimately, Alexander and Oxyartes became allies. Alexander married his daughter Roxane (343–310 B.C.E.) and their marriage helped bring about peace in Bactria and Sogdiana.

In the summer of 327 B.C.E. Alexander returned to Bactria. There he reinforced his troops. He ordered that 30,000 young Persians be formed into an army unit. He also added native cavalry units, including the mounted archers of the Dahae tribe. The addition of so many native soldiers to the army caused great tension among the Macedonian troops.

About two-thirds of the army was ordered to stay to defend Bactria. The rest were sent north to build towns that would serve as garrisons and centers of administration. Hoping to create peace in the region, Alexander encouraged the tribal people to settle in the new towns.

By the spring of 327 B.C.E., Alexander's empire extended along and beyond the southern shores of the Caspian Sea, including modern Afghanistan and Baluchistan, and northward into Bactria and Sogdiana. It had taken him only three years, from the spring of 330 B.C.E. to the spring of 327 B.C.E., to take control of this vast area. Alexander's empire was now almost at its largest.

Despite his desire and efforts to push on to even greater conquests, Alexander added only one more small bit of territory. At its largest, Alexander the Great's empire was 2 million square miles. It stretched from Greece all the way to India.

ANOTHER MURDER PLOT

In the autumn of 327 B.C.E., another murder plot against the new ruler of the Persian Empire was revealed. The would-be assassins were six of his squires, or personal attendants. A total of about 50 young men served as Alexander's squires, and among their duties was guarding the king while he slept.

According to some accounts, on the night of the planned assassination, Alexander stayed up all night drinking and talking with friends. When he found the squires waiting up for him the next morning, he praised what he assumed was their loyalty. Feeling guilty, one of the squires confessed to the murder plot. The Macedonian army found the squires guilty of treason and they were stoned to death.

Other accounts say the squires claimed that Callisthenes (the great-nephew of Alexander's teacher Aristotle) had encouraged their plot. As Alexander's official historian, Callisthenes traveled with the army, compiling an account of events as they occurred. His job was to

To Bow or Not to Bow

Callisthenes and other soldiers were especially critical of Alexander's attempt to introduce the practice of *proskynesis*. This was the eastern custom of bowing to the floor before the Great King. For the Persians bowing to the king was an expression of respect for his royal office. But for the Greeks and Macedonians, bowing was strictly reserved for the gods. They looked upon their king as a fellow warrior, not a god, and had enjoyed an open and equal relationship with Alexander. They hated the idea of bowing down to him now.

Historians have different ideas about why Alexander wanted the soldiers to practice *proskynesis*. Some see it as a sign of his increasing arrogance. He may even have begun to believe himself to be truly a god. Others believe that the Persians might have resented bowing to him when the Macedonians did not. The Persians, whose king was traditionally so high above them, may

have perceived the friendly familiarity of the Macedonians as an indication that the king was not very powerful. All agree that it was difficult for Alexander to be a king to both the Persians and the Macedonians, whose traditions were so different.

One night in the summer of 327 B.C.E., at a banquet in Bactria, Alexander's closest friends convinced the other soldiers to perform *proskynesis*. Only Callisthenes refused to bow. Like Aristotle, he believed strongly in the superiority of Greek culture. Later, he accused Alexander of wanting to be worshipped as a god.

Callisthenes' death did not end his influence. Many important people in Athens were angered about his arrest and subsequent death (although it is not clear how he died). After Alexander's death they wrote hostile and inaccurate accounts about him and joined forces with his enemies in Macedonia.

ensure that by keeping a written record of Alexander's actions, the great conqueror would enjoy widespread fame. Callisthenes also taught some of Alexander's soldiers, including the six squires. Unfortunately, only a few original fragments of his work survive. Most of what we know comes from the writings of others who read Callisthenes and other ancient historians.

Callisthenes' writings reveal his own arrogance. He claimed that Alexander would not win glory as a result of his actions. Rather, he said, Alexander's glory would come from the history of them that Callisthenes wrote. Many of his accounts included ridiculous claims. For example, he wrote that the waves bowed down and worshipped Alexander as he passed the coast.

But at the same time that he was writing these exaggerated accounts of his king's deeds, he was criticizing Alexander in private. Like others, he was critical of Alexander's policy of appointing Persians to high positions. He also did not like the fact that Alexander adopted Persian customs and dress.

It is unclear exactly what became of Callisthenes after the squires' murder plot was uncovered. He was arrested and some historians believe he was then put to death. Others believe that because he was Greek, the Macedonians could not legally try him. They think he was imprisoned and died of a disease some months after his arrest.

TO THE ENDS OF THE EARTH

By the end of 327 b.c.e., many of Alexander's soldiers were beginning to turn against him. The deaths of Philotas and Parmenion, the appointment of Persians to high offices, Alexander adopting Persian customs, his marriage to a Bactrian princess, and the arrest of Callisthenes had all contributed to the general dissatisfaction. Many soldiers assumed the expedition was over and the war was won. They were ready to go home.

But Alexander had other plans. Although his original aim had been to conquer the Persian Empire, he was as much an explorer as a conqueror. Aristotle had taught him about an Encircling Ocean that the Greeks believed surrounded all the lands on earth. Alexander desperately wanted to travel to the ends of the earth and stand on the banks of this ocean. He believed that the best way to reach it was through India. So he pushed his exhausted troops to continue marching east.

CHAPTER 3

FINAL YEARS OF THE EMPIRE

BY THE SUMMER OF 327 B.C.E. ALEXANDER HAD CONQUERED nearly all of the Persian Empire. But instead of focusing on governing his vast domain, he wanted to continue traveling east—to India. He thought that when he reached its eastern edge, he would arrive at the Encircling Ocean.

The historian Arrian claimed that Alexander was motivated by *pothos*, a Greek word that means ambition, curiosity, or a deep longing for something that can never be satisfied. Other historians think he may have been motivated by an ancient legend that said the rulers of India had defeated every foe who ever entered their lands, except for Dionysus, the Greek god, and the mythical hero Heracles. Some historians think the king was simply driven by a lust for war and power.

Whatever Alexander's motivation, most of his troops did not share it. They followed him because they were disciplined soldiers. Some may have also been lured by the hope of finding some of the rare treasures that were said to be in India—a land few people in the West had ever seen.

In the spring of 326 B.C.E., Alexander and his army made the 400-mile trek from Bactria to India. The land that was known as India was not the huge subcontinent it is today, but roughly its northern third. The Macedonians knew little about it. Had they been more familiar with its climate, they probably would not have chosen the beginning of the monsoon season as the time to invade. Monsoons are seasonal heavy rains, and they pour relentlessly for several months. The rains became a greater challenge than the humans Alexander had come to conquer.

OPPOSITE
Alexander (on the left) meets King Porus, who ruled over land that is today a part of northern Punjab in India. After Alexander's victory, he and Porus became great friends. The mural decorates a wall at India House in London, Great Britain.

IN THEIR OWN WORDS

Follow Me!

Alexander was known for making stirring speeches to his troops to inspire them to follow him. The Greek historian Arrian records the following speech Alexander made when he wanted his men to press on into India. Of course, they did.

I observe, gentlemen, that when I would lead you on a new venture you no longer follow me with your old spirit. I have asked you to meet me that we may come to a decision together: are we, upon my advice, to go forward, or, upon yours, to turn back? . . .

I could not have blamed you for being the first to lose heart if I, your commander, had not shared in your exhausting marches and your perilous campaigns; it would have been natural enough if you had done all the work merely for others to reap the reward. But it is not so. You and

I, gentlemen, have shared the labour and shared the danger, and the rewards are for us all. The conquered territory belongs to you; from your ranks the governors of it are chosen; already the greater part of its treasure passes into your hands, and when all Asia is overrun, then indeed I will go further than the mere satisfaction of our ambitions: the utmost hopes of riches or power which each one of you cherishes will be far surpassed, and whoever wishes to return home will be allowed to go, either with me or without me. I will make those who stay the envy of those who return.

(Source: Arrian, "The Speech of Alexander the Great." Ancient History Sourcebook. Available online. URL: http://www.fordham. edu/HALSALL/ancient/arrian-alexander1. htm. Accessed June 1, 2008.)

The first test of Alexander's army came against King Porus (dates unknown), who ruled over land that is today a part of northern Punjab. One of Alexander's allies, a neighboring king, had requested help battling Porus, who was his longtime enemy in the struggle over land rights. Alexander agreed. He confronted Porus at the Hydaspes River (now known as the Jhelum River), which flows though India and Pakistan.

THE BATTLE OF HYDASPES

The Battle of Hydaspes in May 326 B.C.E. is considered one of Alexander's greatest military achievements. The Macedonian leader had to draw on a number of skills: an understanding of psychology, cool nerve, quick reactions, resourcefulness, command of strategy, organizational ability, and leadership. The discipline of his troops was also of critical importance.

As the Hydaspes swelled from the rains, Porus and his army waited on the opposite bank. In addition to his soldiers and archers, he had more than 100 war elephants. Alexander's army built rafts to cross the river. But because the horses were terrified of the elephants, getting them to advance was a challenge. If the horses were even to see the huge beasts during the crossing, it was likely they would jump off the rafts and be swept away by the current.

In pouring rain and thunderstorms, Alexander repeatedly tricked Porus into thinking he was about to attack. He staged large troop movements at crossing points along the river. Night after night, he marched his army along the bank with trumpets blowing. Porus and the elephants would march to meet them on the opposite bank. Then Alexander would retire, leaving the Indians waiting in the rain.

In India, Alexander's army had to come up with new strategies to deal with war elephants. This statue is from the second century B.C.E.

To keep Porus guessing, the Macedonians built up large stores of food and supplies, making it seem that they might be planning to sit out the floods. This made Porus think Alexander was not committed to attacking any time soon. Porus stopped moving his troops every time Alexander moved his. Finally, during a violent thunderstorm on a dark night, the Macedonian army crossed the river. Porus learned of their crossing too late. Catching the Punjabi king's infantry by surprise, the Macedonians immediately killed about half of them.

As he had done in other battles, Alexander avoided a confrontation in the center of the battlefield. He attacked Porus's flank, which forced him to reorganize his forces.

Indian Weaponry

Indian military experts used swords and spears that were handmade from the strongest and highest quality steel—an alloy of iron combined with carbon that had recently been discovered by Indian blacksmiths. They were also equipped with large, powerful bows and six-foot-long arrows. In addition, they trained horses and elephants to fight in wars. Elephants in the Indian army had metal tips fitted to their tusks.

Alexander then took advantage of the Indians' confusion and attacked decisively.

Alexander lost an estimated 1,000 men. Porus lost more than twice that many. Alexander's archers also shot the elephants' mahouts, or drivers. The elephants then trampled the Indian soldiers around them. Many of the Indian soldiers retreated, but Porus fought on. From the back of the tallest elephant, the seven-foot-tall king kept throwing javelins at the Macedonian soldiers, even though he was bleeding from a deep wound.

Alexander sent a messenger to Porus, who surrendered after eight hours of fighting. According to Michael Wood's account in his book *In the Footsteps of Alexander the Great*, when the defeated Porus was asked how he wanted to be treated, he replied, "Treat me like a king."

Alexander was impressed with the Indian king's courage and dignity. He restored Porus's kingdom, and actually enlarged it. The two kings became close friends and Porus's elephant even became an honored hero.

On the site of the battle, Alexander founded two new cities. Both were near Haranpur, in the northern Punjab, northwest of what today is New Delhi, India's capital. One was called Nicaea, which means victory. The other was named Bucephala, in honor of Alexander's treasured horse, Bucephalas, who died shortly after the battle. Alexander had ridden his horse into every one of his battles in Greece and Asia. Bucephalas was 29 when he died—possibly from wounds received at Hydaspes.

TURNING BACK

During June and July the army traveled through the Punjab (it means "land of five rivers") region of India. The soldiers crossed four of the five rivers, and as they went, their difficulties worsened.

Alexander did not often underestimate his human enemies, but in the summer of 326 B.C.E., he did underestimate nature. He had no idea how unbearable the experience of the Indian monsoons would be for his men. For more than two months, it was unbearably hot. The unceasing rain was accompanied by thunder and lighting. Some of the swollen rivers burst their banks and flooded the land around them. The tired soldiers marched through thick mud. Their clothing never had a chance to dry out, and it began to rot and fall apart. To prevent rust they were forced to scrub all their iron equipment daily.

To cross the rivers Alexander's troops made rafts out of their tents by stuffing them with straw. Then they piled their belongings on top. Some soldiers were swept away by the raging waters. Crocodiles that infested the rivers killed others. The rain also caused poisonous snakes to come out of their holes looking for higher ground. Many soldiers died of snakebites.

The unending rain was not the only problem. The soldiers had believed India would be an easy land to conquer. But Porus warned them that ahead of them lay large and powerful kingdoms with huge armies and thousands of elephants.

They also discovered that they were nowhere near Encircling Ocean. After eight hard years of nearly constant marching and combat, the soldiers had little will or energy to go on. The hooves of their horses had been worn thin by steady marching. Even their armor had become nearly useless from wear.

When they reached the fifth and last of the Punjab rivers, the Hyphasis (now the Beas), the soldiers had finally had enough. Alexander pressed them to continue east across the river, but his troops refused. Now clearly aware that their leader was never going to willingly stop marching and fighting, they refused to carry on.

The Macedonian army had a democratic tradition, so the soldiers were acting within their legal rights in refusing. All troops had the right to suggest a plan of action and bring it up for a vote. The king was elected by the army and could also be removed by the army. Alexander had no choice but to go along with their wishes.

Even so, for two days the king tried to change their minds. He threatened to continue on alone. When that failed, he closed himself off inside his tent and spoke to no one. This tactic had worked before to persuade his troops, but not this time.

A soldier named Coenus, who had been the hero of the battle at the Hydaspes, acted as the army's spokesperson. He clearly let Alexander know that his soldiers had had enough and did not want to go on. Finally, Alexander relented. He managed to save his pride when his soothsayers read the omens from the gods that warned against continuing east. By emphasizing that the gods, not the soldiers, had forced him to return, Alexander was also able to maintain his authority. In September 326 B.C.E., for the first time in his military career, Alexander the Great turned back.

A Beloved Horse

As a boy, Alexander tamed a wild horse that no one else had been able to even get near. The young prince named the horse Bucephalas (which means "ox head" because the horse had a natural mark on his coat that was shaped like the head of an ox) and rode him from then on. Years later, while Alexander was battling in the East, bandits snuck into the Macedonians' camp one night and made off with some of their horses. Among them was Alexander's beloved horse. He sent word out to the tribes that Bucephalas must be returned or he would devastate the entire countryside. The thieves returned the now aging horse, for which Alexander rewarded them.

BY LAND AND SEA

For their departure, Alexander had a fleet of 1,800 ships built in just two months. The work was done under the supervision of his admiral and old friend Nearchus (ca. 360–ca. 300 B.C.E.). Carpenters used simple tools to construct both riverboats and ships that could be taken to sea. In November, Nearchus led the fleet south from the Hydaspes River toward the Indus River and the Indian Ocean.

The main part of the army marched alongside the river, at the same pace as the ships. The army, which now included elephants, had to fight hostile groups along the way. They fought with the ferocious Mallians, who lived east of the Acesines (today the Chenab) River. During one fight, Alexander received a serious wound when an arrow pierced his chest.

The army reached the port town of Patala (near modern-day Hyderabad) in July 325 B.C.E. After resting with his troops and exploring some nearby river channels, Alexander began to plan out his return trip to Babylon. First, he instructed a trusted general, Craterus (ca. 362–321 B.C.E.), to take a more northern route to the west. This was the easiest way back. Craterus traveled with the elephants and about a third of the troops, including the older and sick soldiers.

At the same time, Nearchus and nearly 20,000 men set sail west from the mouth of the Indus River. Their plan was to sail up the coast into the Persian Gulf. They explored the northern shore of the Arabian Sea and the Persian Gulf, seeking the mouth of the Tigris and Euphrates Rivers. Today it is not easy to reconstruct their voyage, because it was not possible at that time to measure distances at sea.

Many historians believe the fleet took this route to open up a sea trade route between Persia and India. To accomplish this, they would have had to chart the coast and make maps of landing sites and wells. In fact, trading routes did open up or were reinforced after this voyage. One important trade route linked western India to port cities in Egypt via the Red Sea.

DEATH IN THE DESERT

Alexander himself marched his remaining army of 30,000 men west to Turbat, Pakistan. Then, instead of continuing west, he headed south toward the Indian Ocean. The plan was for Alexander to meet up with Nearchus at a meeting point along the coast, and probably again at various points along the way westward. The fleet would supply the land troops with grain and provisions and the troops would provide wells and protection for the fleet whenever it needed to come ashore for fresh water.

The army set out before the fleet, marched to the coast, and reached the meeting point. There, the troops waited on land for Nearchus's ships. But they never showed up. No one knew why. They later discovered the ships had waited an extra week for the monsoons to die down and were further delayed by strong winds that blew straight into their path.

The soldiers had been depending on the fleet to supply them with food. The region was bare and not much grew, and soon they used up the available food supplies. They could not return the way they had come, because they had stripped the land through which they had just traveled. Without food, they could not remain at the meeting point to wait for the fleet, especially since they feared it had been destroyed by a storm or an enemy attack.

Alexander decided to lead his army inland, rather than continue along the coast. He did not know that this meant they would march through the worst part of the desert. His decision not to return to Turbat and go west from there was not a fortunate one. In the end, it took the army through miles of some of the world's worst deserts. These included the Makran Desert that borders the

Desert Dangers

Alexander meant to meet up with his fleet and its commander, Nearchus, at either Pasni or Gwadar, but that mission failed. The troops were left to make a death-defying trek west across the desolate Makran Desert and up into the Gedrosian Desert. From Pasni, it took days by camel train to reach the scorched seaside village of Gwadar, where Alexander dug wells.

Today the westward trip might take three days at least. The landscape still looks as bare as the moon. There is no fresh water to be found between the two towns. Along the way, stark, dry ridges stick up into the sky. Deep, drifting sand dunes make walking nearly impossible and camels are the only practical means of transportation. There is very little plant life. The sun burns and rain rarely falls. At a place called Sur Bandar, crude straw huts hug the shore and the boats of fishermen dot the sea's surface—the only hint of a more modern world.

The modern world is apparent, however, in today's Pasni and Gwadar. Gwadar is striving to become a major seaport as big as its neighbor to the east, Karachi, Pakistan. Pasni today is well-known to the United States Army. Since the September 11, 2001, terrorist attacks, the military and allied forces have been using Pasni's commercial airport as an air base—as they also did during World War II.

north end of the Indian Ocean, as well as the region of Gedrosia, which lies northwest of the Makran.

As with so many other events of Alexander's career, historians disagree about many aspects of this march. They are not sure whether Alexander knew how difficult this crossing would be. Some believe he did know and wanted to prove that his army could do what others had failed to accomplish. Others believe he had no idea and that local guides who were hostile to the Macedonians may have intentionally misinformed them. Other historians believe the disaster was the result of an unfortunate series of events and that Alexander's legendary luck finally failed him.

Alexander began his desert march with somewhere between 10,000 and 70,000 people. As always, women, children, craftsmen, and others traveled with the soldiers. The march took about two months, and three-quarters of them died along the way. All suffered severely from starvation, thirst, and disease. Flash floods and poisonous snakes wiped out many. Those who were too sick and exhausted to continue were left behind to die. Alexander shared these hardships. Often, to set an example, he dismounted from his horse and walked.

It is believed that more soldiers died from hunger and thirst during the crossing of the Gedrosian Desert than in all of Alexander's battles in Asia. But finally, at the end of 325 B.C.E., the survivors reached Carmania in eastern Persia (today's Kerman in south central Iran). There they reunited with Nearchus's fleet and Craterus's troops. There was a great celebration.

REBUILDING AN EMPIRE

Alexander returned to Susa early in 324 B.C.E. He discovered that some parts of the Persian Empire had started to rebel during his Indian campaigns. Several satraps had recruited private armies and had been abusing their powers. They acted as if they expected Alexander would never return.

Alexander took quick and decisive steps to regain control. He executed the rebellious satraps. He also executed a number of soldiers from the garrison of Media (now part of northwest Iran) who had looted temples and tombs. Persian rebel leaders who had been captured by Craterus were also executed.

At the same time, the newly returned king began a number of projects aimed at improving trade and expanding the empire's routes of commerce. He had wells dug in dry areas and ordered the building of roads and bridges that could be used in all weather conditions. (Unfortunately, these plans were not completed before his death and were abandoned afterward when others took control of his lands.) He gave large rewards to surviving soldiers who had remained loyal to him. He also repaid the debts many of his soldiers had incurred.

In an attempt to unite his eastern and western subjects, in March 324 B.C.E. Alexander organized a mass marriage. He had about 90 of his military officers marry daughters of Persian aristocrats. A fabulous banquet was held for 9,000 people. The event was intended to develop a greater spirit of cooperation between Macedonians and Persians.

Alexander set an example by taking his second and third wives—first Parysatis (dates unknown) and then Stateira (ca. 340–320 B.C.E.), Darius's daughter. Marrying Stateira strengthened his claim to kingship of the Persian Empire. Alexander's closest companion, Hephaestion, married another of Darius's daughters. Alexander also offered a monetary reward to soldiers who married Persian wives. About 10,000 of his men took advantage of the offer.

In another bold move, the king announced that he was releasing older and injured Macedonian veterans from military service. He replaced them with 30,000 Persian young men who had been studying the Greek language and Macedonian methods of fighting. The army still considered the Persians to be barbarians and protested. They said if anyone was dismissed, they would all leave.

In response, their ruler again made a stirring speech. He reminded the soldiers of their glorious victories under him. Then he asked them to consider themselves citizens of a larger empire, and said he made no distinction between Greeks and barbarians. The speech, sometimes called the Oath of Alexander, turned things around yet again. The soldiers withdrew their threat of mutiny.

Alexander discharged about 10,000 men and gave them large bonuses. He provided them with extra money to return to Greece and promised to educate their Persian children. He also had 13 of his most outspoken critics executed without a trial.

Alexander integrated new troops that arrived from Macedon with the Persian soldiers. The Macedonians were placed in the front with spears and the Persians, carrying swords and javelins, marched in rows behind them.

The main purpose of integrating Macedonians and Persians in the army (and also of the mass marriages) was to replace Macedonians with Asians for military and administrative purposes. In addition, the children born of such unions would be of mixed blood with loyalty to no one but their commander in chief, Alexander.

DEATH OF HEPHAESTION

In October 324 B.C.E. Alexander's dearest friend, Hephaestion, became ill and died in Ecbatana. Alexander was devastated by the death and ordered Hephaestion's doctor to be killed. Then he sat with his best friend's body for three days, never leaving his side.

Alexander spent a fortune on a very grand funeral. It included 3,000 participants in the traditional funeral games, which included contests in literature and athletics. Alexander took his example from the funeral games described in the *Iliad*. They were organized by the great hero Achilles for his friend Patroclus, who was killed in the Trojan War.

After this loss, Alexander's health began to decline. Many of his war injuries started to bother him. Some historians believe he had become an alcoholic by this time. Frequent drinking bouts may have further undermined his health.

It was at this time that Alexander asked the Greeks to give him the status of a god. Although this honor was sometimes granted to Greek rulers after their death, most people, including Alexander's soldiers and the Greeks back home, found the king's request absurd. Some of his countrymen thought Alexander was going insane. Even his teacher Aristotle criticized him openly.

The funeral Alexander arranged for Hephaestion was modeled after the funeral the great Greek hero Achilles had for his friend Patroclus, which is shown here. Achilles and Patroclus were warriors in the Greek epic the *Iliad*.

Legendary Friendship

Alexander met Hephaestion when they were boys in Macedonia. The two friends studied together with Aristotle and remained extremely close during their entire lives. Alexander and Hephaestion saw themselves as being much like Achilles and his dear friend Patroclus, whose brave deeds were chronicled in the *Iliad*.

In ancient Greek culture, sexual relations were common among male friends and it would not have been unusual for them to be lovers. There was no word in the ancient Greek language for homosexual or bisexual, because the Greeks did not group people by sexual preference.

Alexander's name for Hephaestion was Philalexandros—"friend of Alexander." Hep-haestion's great rival, the general Craterus, only rated the title of Philobasileus, "friend of the king."

Hephaestion was not a great military leader, but probably had talents for diplomacy and logistics (coordinating complex operations). Although some historians have portrayed him as a man who always agreed with his king, it is more likely that he had great freedom to speak truthfully to Alexander. This is partly because he had different skills than Alexander and so they did not compete.

At the time of his death in Ecbatana in 324 B.C.E., Hephaestion was the second most powerful man in Alexander's empire. Alexander died just eight months after his life-long companion.

Nevertheless, the Greeks ultimately granted the request, probably because of all the money Alexander had sent them. But their ongoing criticism of him at home showed they did not really believe he was a god.

THE BUSINESS OF RUNNING AN EMPIRE

In April 323 B.C.E., Alexander returned to Babylon. He planned to establish the city as the capital of his empire. There, for the first time, he devoted himself to the administration of his vast empire, which stretched from Greece to India.

He had high hopes for his empire. He wanted to create the kind of government that Aristotle described as the ideal—rule by a "philosopher king." He encouraged his subjects to feel that they were citizens of a united world, rather than just members of their own nation or culture. He wanted to establish an era of cooperation.

He also hoped to unite and strengthen his empire by developing a common culture—Greek culture, although with some Persian influences. He gave his new Persian soldiers instruction in Greek literature. And while he adopted some Persian customs, he also encouraged his eastern subjects to become more like the Greeks and Macedonians.

Alexander had many other ambitious plans. He believed that commerce would help unite his empire, and he intended to make Babylon its commercial center. He laid plans to build docks along the Euphrates River at Babylon and to clear the river all the way to the Persian Gulf. He also planned to start colonies along the eastern shore of the Persian Gulf and to explore Arabia. He may have been preparing to invade Arabia and, from there, to conquer the entire North African coast.

DEATH AT 32

Alexander never saw his grand hopes and plans fulfilled. In the early summer of 323 B.C.E. he became ill. About 10 days later, on June 10, just before his 33rd birthday and nearly 13 years after becoming the king of Macedon, Alexander died.

The similarity between his death and Hephaestion's led to suspicions that both were poisoned. Some historians suggested that Alexander's cupbearer—the servant who gave him his wine—might have been the culprit. His father, Antipater (ca. 398–319 B.C.E.), was a senior Macedonian official. By this time in his life there was no shortage of enemies or rivals who would have wanted to see Alexander dead.

However, most historians today agree that Alexander died from disease. The most recent scholarship suggests it was an infectious disease, perhaps typhoid fever. It was made worse by physical and mental stress, multiple wounds, malaria, occasional heavy drinking, and exhaustion.

Even though many soldiers had become disillusioned with Alexander, most still loved their leader. They sat outside his tent as his condition deteriorated. The day before he died his soldiers marched past his deathbed, honoring their great leader. The ancient Greek historian Arrian claimed that despite his pain and weak condition, Alexander made eye contact with each of his men as they marched past.

Alexander's remarkable 13-year reign carved out his place in history. But the great conqueror failed to establish a stable empire. Although his first wife, Roxane, was pregnant with a son at the time of her husband's death, Alexander the Great did not designate a successor—the person to rule after him. In the last moments of the great king's life, his generals asked him to whom he wanted to leave his empire. Many sources (quoted in *In the Footsteps of Alexander the Great* by Michael Wood) say Alexander's deathbed reply was, "*to kratisto*"—to the strongest.

One of Alexander's great strengths was that he understood the men who served under him. He predicted that his generals would fight one other for control of his kingdom, and he was right. The intrigue and ferocious power struggles among the *diadochi*, or successors, would last for more than a generation.

After Alexander's death, the Macedonians spent a year creating a magnificent funeral carriage. His body was preserved and placed in a solid gold coffin, which was carried under a golden, jewel-encrusted model of a temple. A gold statue of the Greek goddess of victory, Nike, stood on the roof of the carriage.

At the funeral march, his soldiers followed the carriage, which was pulled by 64 mules wearing golden bells. Road builders went ahead of the spectacular funeral train. As the procession traveled west across 1,000 miles of Asia its fame spread. Crowds gathered in every city along the way to watch the procession pass.

The destination of Alexander's body was Macedon, but it never reached his home. Ptolemy (372–283 B.C.E.), Alexander's friend and the new ruler of Egypt, grabbed the carriage and took it to Alexandria. There it was placed in a special tomb. The exact location of Alexander's tomb, like so many

CONNECTIONS

Intrigue in Alexandria

Alexander's coffin was first buried in the Egyptian capital of Memphis. Later, it was reburied at the center of ancient Alexandria. That spot was known as the Sema, a word that referred to the place where Alexander's mausoleum was located. It was the place where the city's two grandest streets—lined with columns and each reportedly 200 feet wide—crossed. But as the city grew, its center shifted and knowledge of the tomb's exact location was lost. The last record of its whereabouts is dated in the fourth century C.E. So far, the ongoing search for Alexander's tomb has found nothing.

Recent underwater excavations in Alexandria's old harbor have provided promising clues. Archaeologists now believe that the search should take place much farther east in the city than originally thought. They say the old city center was probably in the region of what is now a cemetery dating from the 19th century. Intriguing evidence has actually been found in the area they suggest. This includes the outer chamber of a royal tomb designed in the Macedonian style and made from high-quality alabaster—a beautiful white stone.

of the facts of his life, is hotly debated. Many archaeologists have tried to find it, and some still search for it today.

THREE KINGDOMS

Alexander turned out to be the only individual whose personal authority could hold his huge empire together. Some of his followers, including the ordinary soldiers of the Macedonian army, wanted to preserve the empire. But with no successor named and no stable kingship to maintain what he had won, the empire immediately began falling apart.

Alexander's generals all wanted to carve out huge kingdoms for themselves. The power conflict among them lasted about 40 years, from 323 to 280 B.C.E. Through struggles and warfare, three generals— Ptolemy, Seleucus (ca. 358–281 B.C.E.), and Antigonus (ca. 382–301 B.C.E.)—emerged as powerful contenders. At first, Antigonus was the most powerful of the new kings. But he was defeated at the battle of Ipsos in 301 B.C.E. This battle among the kings put an end to all hopes of reunifying Alexander's empire.

From each of these three generals, a major dynasty (a family that keeps control of a government over many generations) emerged. The Ptolemies controlled what had been the Egyptian Empire (Egypt, Syria, Cyprus, the Aegean Islands, and parts of Asia Minor). The Seleucids ruled what had been the Persian Empire, and the Antigonids became rulers in Macedon and Greece. Eventually, all three kingdoms were overtaken by the military might of the Roman Empire.

The Egyptian Empire of Ptolemy was the richest, most powerful, and most stable of the kingdoms—as well as the longest lasting of the three. Alexandria became its capital. Ptolemy lived to an old age, and his kingdom was the last dynasty of the Egyptian kings known as pharaohs. Egypt reached its height of material and cultural splendor under Ptolemy II Philadelphus, who ruled from 285 to 246 B.C.E. After his death, a long period of war and internal fighting followed. In 30 B.C.E., the death of the famous Queen Cleopatra VII, Ptolemy's descendant, marked the end of Hellenistic rule in the region. (Hellenistic means based on Greek culture.) Egypt became a province of the Roman Empire.

Seleucus, who was given the nickname "the conqueror," grabbed the largest territory. But he was murdered before he could achieve his

Who Is Buried in King Philip's Tomb?

In 1977, archaeologists announced an exciting discovery: They had found what they believed to be the tomb of Alexander's father, King Philip II of Macedon. The tomb was located in what is now Vergina, Greece. The objects in the tomb, which included a gold *larnax*, or ancient Greek casket, a magnificent set of armor, and a gold wreath, came from the fourth century B.C.E. The lid of the *larnax* was decorated with a starburst, which was the emblem of the Macedonian royal family.

The body in the tomb had been cremated, but the bones had been

This tomb was once thought to be the burial place of Alexander's father, King Philip II.

carefully wrapped in a purple cloth. Scientists were able to use pieces of the skull to reconstruct the face, and they discovered that the right side of the face was distorted. This provided further evidence that the body was that of King Philip II, since it was known that an injury had caused him to lose his right eye.

More recent research has revealed that the tomb is most likely not that of Alexander's father, however, but of Alexander's half-brother, Philip III Arrhidaeus. Scientists were able to more closely date the objects in the tomb. They discovered they were from approximately 317 B.C.E., the year Philip III died. Using a technique called macrophotography, they were able to study the skeleton in greater detail than had been possible when the tomb was first discovered. They determined that the distortions believed to have been caused by the loss of an eye were actually caused by the effects of cremation and reassembly of the bones.

ambition of seizing the throne of Macedon as well. His kingdom was continued by his heirs. At its largest, the Seleucid Empire stretched from the Aegean Sea to Central Asia.

Lasting Influence

Alexander's death marked the end of what historians call the classical, or Hellenic, period of Greek history. (*Hellas* is the word the Greeks used to mean the entire Greek world and is what Greeks today call their nation.) The Greek city-states never regained their former greatness, but their culture continued to spread far and wide. Greek ideas about politics, language, learning, culture, art, and philosophy affected the way many civilizations subsequently developed. This era after Alexander died is known as the Hellenistic period. Hellenistic culture ultimately was spread throughout the east and west by the Roman Empire, which greatly admired the Greeks.

The Seleucid dynasty founded the most new cities of any monarchy in history. The Seleucids established many Greek settlements throughout their lands, and their empire lasted more than 241 years. By 129 B.C.E., the Seleucid Empire included Palestine, Syria, and Persia. But it continually lost territory over the years because of wars and rebellions, and slowly crumbled to pieces. The empire's decline continued as the Parthians, a nomadic tribe from central Asia, gradually captured all of its territories east of Syria. Its western areas were taken over by the Roman Empire in 64 B.C.E.

The Antigonid kingdom of Macedon was continuously involved in wars with other kingdoms and struggles with the Greek city-states. Because Alexander had drained Macedon of much of its manpower, it was the smallest and poorest of the three kingdoms. Although it was weak, this empire remained prestigious as Alexander's homeland.

Immediately after the death of Alexander, the generals appointed two kings of Macedon. One was Philip III Arrhidaeus (ca. 352–317 B.C.E.), son of Philip II and half-brother of Alexander. The other was Alexander IV (323–310 B.C.E.), Roxane's son, who was an infant at the time. They ruled jointly until Arrhidaeus's murder in 317 B.C.E.

Ultimately, the ruthless Cassander (358–297 B.C.E.) became king of Macedon in 305 B.C.E. Cassander was the son of Antipater, the regent of Macedon during Alexander's campaigns in Persia. To help pave his way to the throne, Cassander married Alexander's half-sister, Thessalonice (346–298 B.C.E.). He had Alexander's mother killed in 316 B.C.E. In 310 B.C.E. he executed Alexander's widow Roxane and his son, Alexander IV, who was then 13 years old.

In the great struggle for control in the years after Alexander's death, many others were killed too. These included several of the king's generals, his sister, his half-brother, his sister-in-law, and a nephew.

PART · II

SOCIETY AND CULTURE

SOCIETY IN ALEXANDER'S EMPIRE

LIVING IN ALEXANDER'S EMPIRE

ART, SCIENCE, AND CULTURE ACROSS THE EMPIRE

CHAPTER 4

SOCIETY IN ALEXANDER'S EMPIRE

THE PHILOSOPHER ARISTOTLE ADVISED ALEXANDER TO "play the part of a leader to the Greeks, and of a master to the barbarians, and to care for the former as friends and kinsmen, and treat the latter as beasts and plants" (as quoted by Dutch scholar and author Jona Lendering). This view of foreigners as barbarians inferior to the Greeks was shared by most of Aristotle's countrymen.

Aristotle's most famous student did not agree with this outlook. Alexander came to have a great deal of respect for his eastern subjects, and even began to adopt many of their customs. Eventually, Alexander's respect for the Persians became a source of conflict between him and his army, even his closest generals. But he never changed his mind.

As a result of Alexander's conquests Greek culture spread throughout the Middle East. His death marks the beginning of what has become known as the Hellenistic period, which lasted for about 300 years. The term *Hellenism* is typically used to describe the influence of Greece on the East, and most scholars have focused on how Greek culture affected the rest of the world. The influence flowed both ways, though. There was a great deal of exchange between east and west, and Greek society was also influenced by Persia during the Hellenistic period.

There were many similarities between Greek and Persian society. Both had strong divisions between their upper and lower classes. Both accepted slavery. Women and children had virtually no rights in either society.

However, in many ways the two societies were very different. The Greeks worshipped many gods, while most Persians believed in a single god. The Greeks spoke one language. The Persian Empire included

Hunting was considered an essential part of any young Macedonian prince's education. Alexander loved riding and hunting, and even arranged hunts during his military campaigns. He is shown here in a mosaic hunting lions.

many different nationalities with different languages. More than a dozen languages were spoken in Asia Minor alone.

The governments of Greece and Persia were very different. Greece was not an empire with a single ruler. Rather, it was a collection of city-states that functioned much like separate nations. Each had its own government, laws, and customs. Some, including Athens, were democracies. Some were oligarchies (where power was shared by a wealthy aristocracy). And some, such as Sparta, were monarchies with a king. Although the Greek city-states sometimes united to fight a common enemy, they functioned as separate states. Persia was a unified monarchy, with a single, central ruler.

MACEDON: KINGDOM WITH SHARED POWER

Macedon, Alexander's homeland, was just north of Greece. Macedon was a monarchy. But unlike the Persian Empire, where the king had absolute power, the power of the Macedonian king was limited. His primary responsibilities were administrative and military. He was also in charge of official religious functions. For example, he performed state sacrifices daily—and Alexander did too, every day until his death. The king was also the final judge in any legal appeal.

The king shared his power with the Macedonian assembly. The assembly was a powerful group made up of Macedonian citizens. Among other responsibilities, it judged cases of treason (the crime of betraying one's country). Although the king and the assembly were supposed to share equally in the government of Macedon, in reality the king had more power than the assembly.

Macedonian had an aristocracy (a small group of the highest-ranking people), but it was not based entirely on birth. All men who were in service to the king had an equal opportunity to rise to the highest levels. The king chose his Companions—the elite group of soldiers who served him directly—based on personal quality and loyalty rather than on family background or connections. However, the aristocratic families controlled large groups of followers, which meant the king needed their support to continue ruling effectively. The most powerful aristocrats were considered the king's social equals.

In Macedon, the king was expected to listen to his people. The Macedonian people were traditionally allowed to address the king with a great deal of freedom. A soldier addressing the king in the assembly

IN THEIR OWN WORDS

A Typical Day

In this section of his book *Lives*, the Greek historian Plutarch describes a typical day for Alexander during his initial invasion of Persia. Even while on a military campaign, Alexander did many of the things any young Macedonian prince did, including hunting, drinking, and performing the daily sacrifice.

He had less of a penchant for wine than was generally thought. He gained this reputation because he dragged out the time he took over each cup, but it was time spent talking rather than drinking, since he was constantly presiding over some lengthy conversation or other, at any rate when he had plenty of time. When action was called for, unlike other commanders he was not detained by wine, sleep, some trivial pursuit or other, marriage, or a show—as is proved by his life, which for all its brevity is packed with exploit after major exploit. When he had time on his hands, however, he would get up and sacrifice to the gods,

and then immediately sit down to eat his morning meal. Then he would go on to spend the day hunting or arranging his affairs or teaching some aspect of warfare or reading. If he was on a leisurely journey he would try to improve his archery during it, or practice mounting and dismounting from a moving chariot; as we can learn from the Royal Diary, he also often used to hunt foxes and birds for fun. Once he had found quarters for the night, he would ask his bakers and cooks, while he was busy with bathing or washing, whether they had everything they needed for his evening meal. He used to take to his couch and eat his evening meal late, after dark, and take an astonishing amount of care and consideration at the table to make sure that everyone got equal—and equally generous—portions.

(Source: Plutarch, *Greek Lives*. Translated by Robin Waterfield. New York: Oxford University Press, 1999.)

would have to uncover his head. But whatever his rank, he could speak openly and frankly.

One of the most important responsibilities of a new king was to create successors as soon as possible. For this reason, many Macedonian kings had more than one wife. They were also expected to train their potential successors in the arts of hunting and warfare.

Fighting within the royal family had always been common in Macedon. There had also traditionally been disputes among the leading aristocrats. Macedonian kings were therefore never really safe, even in their own palaces. Power struggles often led to plotting, intrigue, and assassination. It became a custom for the kings to station guards both outside and inside the door to their bedroom.

This relief carved at the Palace at Persepolis shows Persian king Xerxes entering his grand hall. Great ceremonies surrounded everything the king did.

Because the Macedonian kingship was so unstable, princes typically married soon after they turned 20. This was much earlier than other men in that society. The idea was to get started on making a family as soon as possible, in the likely event that a successor to the king became necessary.

When Alexander became king at the age of 20, his advisors tried to convince him to marry and have a child before leaving to invade Persia. He should have taken their advice, since the lack of a clear successor was a major reason why his empire fell apart after his death. It is quite possible, however, that even if Alexander had a son before leaving Macedon, rivals would have killed the prince.

PERSIA: POWERFUL MONARCHY

The king of the Persian Empire was known as the Great King or King of Kings. He ruled by divine right (a right conferred by God) and exercised complete control over his subjects. The only limits to his enormous power were that he was expected to follow Persia's customs and was required to consult the highest-ranking nobles before making any important decisions. Because of the king's power these nobles often simply agreed with him, no matter what he said.

Although the Persians did not regard their king as a god, everything about him was meant to emphasize his greatness and superiority. Many ceremonies, rules, and customs were associated with the king and his court. He wore purple robes and sat on an elaborately decorated throne. His servants were required to hold their hands in front of their mouths in the king's presence so that he would not have to breathe the same air they did. He walked on red carpets that were put out only for him. In sculptures the king was always shown larger than everyone else.

The king provided a meal each day for about 15,000 aristocrats, courtiers (a person at the royal court who is a companion to the king), and other subjects. This was meant to show his concern for his loyal subjects. It also showed off his enormous wealth. The king himself was hidden from the view of his guests when he ate.

All of the king's subjects, including the highest aristocrats, were expected to kneel before the king and bow their foreheads to the ground. This practice was called *proskynesis*. *Proskynesis* is an example of the kind of cultural difference that existed between east and west. In the later years of his reign Alexander tried to convince his army to practice this custom and bow down to him, but most of them would not accept it.

GREECE: FREEDOM FOR SOME

Many forms of government emerged in Greece's many city-states. One of them was democracy, where all the citizens had equal rights. One of the most important ideas that has been handed down by the ancient Greeks is that of democracy. Citizens had the freedom to think and to speak as they wished and the right to choose their public officials.

CONNECTIONS

Greek Politics

Many of the political ideals we cherish today came from the Greeks. The word *politics* comes from the Greek word *polis*, usually translated as "city-state." The word *democracy* comes from the Greek word *demokratia*, which means "the power of people."

When Greek civilization began, authority was based on brute force—as it was in most of the ancient world. But the Greeks were the first to ask what the role of a government should be. Some Greek philosophers decided that the state should exist for the benefit of its citizens. Therefore, they reasoned, those citizens had the right to help make decisions. They believed that it was not just a right, but also a duty of every citizen to participate in the government.

Citizens had legal and political rights, and could own land. However, only one out of every six residents was a citizen.

There was social and economic inequality in the Greek city-states, even the democracies. Wealthy citizens had more opportunities and advantages. And there were high-status and low-status occupations.

There were also inequalities between the citizens and the other two types of residents: foreigners and slaves. Foreigners had no political rights. If a foreigner stayed in a city for longer than a specified period of time, he had to register as a resident alien and pay a tax. Resident aliens might be artisans, merchants, or bankers. They could become wealthy, but with very rare exceptions, they could never become citizens. However, they also were in no danger of ending up as slaves.

There was also inequality between male and female citizens. For example, Athens, Greece's most prominent democracy, was a highly patriarchal society. This means that the father controlled the family.

Women did not have the same political rights as men. Girl babies were not even fed as well as boys. Women did not have the right to attend political assemblies or to vote. With few exceptions, they were not allowed to participate in public events at all—not even dinner parties.

Women could not own, inherit, or manage property, or take part in any business deal in which something worth more than a bushel of grain was exchanged. Poor women worked, however, as dressmakers, weavers, and midwives (people who help women give birth).

A woman had to have an official male guardian to protect her physically and legally. Citizen women could take a legal dispute to court, but they had to have men speak for them. Women had authority only over children and slaves. A woman was responsible for cooking, housework, and spinning and weaving cloth for the family's clothing.

Wealthy married women were practically prisoners in their homes. They could not leave the house except to visit relatives, attend marriages and funerals, and participate in certain religious festivals. A wife sometimes shopped at the market for small purchases. But when women went out, they were required to have a male servant or slave accompany them.

In reality, only wealthy husbands could afford to keep their wives this way. Women in families with less money might have stalls at the market where they sold goods, and they did their own shopping. But isolation was considered the ideal.

Persia was also a patriarchal society, although Persian women had greater freedom than Athenian women. They took care of the home and were encouraged to have as many children as possible, so that the king's army would always be supplied with soldiers. They were not allowed to see any men other than their husbands. Unlike Greek women, however, they were permitted to own property and could conduct business from their homes.

Women in Alexander's time had many jobs, but little power. Raising children was among their most important roles.

CLASS SYSTEMS THROUGHOUT THE EMPIRE

The Greeks, the Macedonians, and the Persians all had class systems. The upper classes of Macedonian society admired the Greeks. The Macedonians had their own language, which may have been similar to Greek, but the upper classes also spoke Greek. They considered themselves to be Greek by blood. At the same time, Macedon was a rough land with a colder climate, and the Macedonians looked down on their southern Greek neighbors as softer and less sturdy than themselves.

The Greeks thought even less highly of the Macedonians. They considered Macedon a crude, remote place whose people were little better than barbarians.

Babbling Barbarians

Aristotle, like all the Greeks of his time, believed people who did not speak his language were uncivilized *barbaroi*, not deserving of any status much better than slave. The Greek word *barbaroi*, the root of the English word *barbarian*, is translated as "babbler" or "jabberer." So all non-Greeks were considered nothing but babblers.

There were some significant differences between the culture of Macedon and that of the rest of Greece. Even though Macedon was a male-dominated society, the queens and royal mothers were greatly respected. This was largely because they came from powerful Macedonian families or from ruling families in neighboring lands. They were given respect because they gave birth to the successor their husbands needed for their royal dynasties to continue. When the king was away, the royal women sometimes engaged in power struggles with the king's male representatives, as Alexander's mother did.

The favorite pastimes of the Macedonian upper classes were fighting, hunting, and heavy drinking. The king could only gain respect from the nobility if he was an expert in all these activities. This was seen as an indication that he would be capable of heading the state. Hunting on horseback was seen as a useful aspect of military training. Alexander loved riding and hunting, and before he became king he probably hunted almost every day. He stalked animals such as bears, lions, and deer that roamed the hills of Macedon.

Persian society was divided into two classes. We know more today about the lifestyle of Persia's upper classes than about its lower classes. The upper class included the king, the aristocracy, and the priests.

At the head of the upper class was the king. Just below him in power were his chief aristocrats. They served as officers and cavalry in the army. The lower class included the majority of Persians, who were laborers. Freemen got paid and could choose where they worked. Bondsmen were serfs and slaves, and had little or no choice about where and for whom they worked.

However, actual Persians were a tiny minority in the Persian Empire. The vast majority of others in the empire lived according to their own customs. Locally, they had great freedom to arrange their society according to their traditions.

All of the land in Persia belonged to the king. But the kings gave land holdings to aristocrats and military leaders. These lands were named in military terms, according to their size. For example, there were "bow," "horse," and "chariot" lands, and the owners of these lands had to provide men and equipment for the army accordingly. One of the smallest parcels, a bow land, was about 52 acres and its lord was expected to supply one archer to the army. Some lords had parcels of many thousands of acres and had to provide much greater numbers of men and equipment.

SERFS AND SLAVES

Maintaining these estates required a lot of work. Serfs lived on a Persian aristocrat's estate and worked in exchange for some of the crops. These serfs were considered part of the property on which they worked. They were expected to fight for the lord who owned the land, if necessary. If the land changed hands, the serfs and their families remained with it.

Slaves, unlike serfs, could be sold. They were often more highly skilled than serfs. Many were prisoners of war who performed the same trades they had performed before they were captured.

In most of Greece there were no serfs (Sparta was one exception), but there were slaves. Slaves were considered to be their owners' property. They had few rights and could have no family or possessions. Slaves could, however, buy or inherit their freedom.

People ended up as slaves for many reasons. Children who were abandoned by their parents often became slaves. So did enemy soldiers who had been captured. Captives were rarely killed because they were valuable to their captors. How captives were treated depended on whether their families were rich or poor. Rich captives were often sold back to their families, while poor captives typically became slaves. Alexander sent many captured soldiers back to Greece and Macedon to become slaves.

The lives of most slaves were probably not too different from those of farm workers or servants. An exception was slaves who had to dig in the silver mines in Athens and Macedon. Their lives were extremely difficult.

THE VAST PERSIAN EMPIRE

The Persian Empire had an ancient, advanced culture. From about 550 B.C.E. until Alexander's time, the Persian Empire was ruled by a dynasty called the Achaemenids. The first and greatest of the Achaemenid kings was Darius I. His rule, which began in 522 B.C.E., began what is known as the Achaemenid era. It continued until Alexander conquered the empire.

By the time Darius I came to power, the Persian Empire had expanded to include a vast territory of diverse populations. It stretched from what is now Turkey in the west to what is now Afghanistan and India in the east. Its northern boundary was the southern part of Turkmenistan and Uzbekistan, and in the south it extended to Egypt and the Indian Ocean.

The Persian Empire was the largest, most powerful, and wealthiest empire in the world. The kingdom was nearly 5,000 miles wide from east to west, wider than the continental United States. It encompassed a total of 15 modern countries and spanned parts of three continents.

The Persian Empire united people and kingdoms from every major civilization of the time, except China. Its many regions had different traditions, laws, economic conditions, languages, religions, and cultures. All were brought together under one ruler for the first time. At its height, the empire had about 40 million people.

Although Persia was a monarchy, its enormous size made it impossible for one person to govern it effectively. Darius I therefore divided his lands into 20 huge districts, called satrapies. Many satrapies were large enough to constitute kingdoms themselves. Each satrapy was ruled by a local governor, called a satrap.

Satraps were chosen mainly from the Persian aristocracy. Many were members of the Persian royal family or trusted friends. A satrap was a powerful figure who ruled over his province like a king. However, the true kings put measures in place to keep the satraps from having too much power. For example, they put army officers in charge of the military forces stationed in the satrapy and appointed other officials to collect the taxes. The kings also sent out royal inspectors to keep an eye on the satraps and the other officials.

When Alexander conquered the empire, he allowed most of the satraps and other Persian officials to remain in positions of authority. He usually gave administrative power to the Persians and gave the Macedonians control over the military and the treasury. He also gave the common people the right to make a direct appeal to the king for the first time.

The Persian Empire became rich, partly through the taxes the kings collected. The annual tax typically amounted to about 10 percent of the people's resources. It could be paid in the form of precious metals, food, or other commodities. Taxes were collected in different ways in different areas. Money was also collected from rulers of nearby lands in order to preserve peace.

For nearly 200 years before Alexander, the Persians held an annual festival on their New Year's Day, which was the spring equinox (the first day of spring). It was called the Festival of the Tribute. Representatives from all parts of the empire would come to the magnificent royal palace at Persepolis for this grand occasion, bringing lavish gifts for the king. The king held court in a great hall whose ceiling was supported by 100

A Tent Fit for a King

One key difference between the Macedonians and the Persians was the lavish wealth of Persian royalty. Alexander, who lived much more simply than the Persian kings, was amazed by the royal tent left behind when Darius III fled from the battlefield at the Battle of Issus. It contained a golden throne and bath, gold and silver drinking cups, carpets, jewels, and other treasures. The historians Arrian and Quintus Curtius Rufus give an account of Alexander's reaction to this fantastic wealth. Alexander remarked (as related in Michael Wood's book *In the Footsteps of Alexander the Great*), "So this is what it is like to be a king."

Another key difference was the way royalty was addressed in the two cultures. Alexander entered the tent with his close friend, Hephaestion. Darius's mother, Sisygambis, had been left behind when Darius fled. Seeing the two men, she assumed that Hephaestion, the taller and thus more impressive man by Persian standards, must be the king. So she addressed him as "Alexander." Learning of her mistake, she became afraid, possibly believing that such an insult would cost her life. Many sources (including Robin Lane Fox in his book *Alexander the Great*) provide Alexander's legendary reply. "Do not worry," Alexander told Sisygambis, "He, too, is Alexander."

columns. As part of a great ceremony, they would wait in their national dress until they were brought in to see the king and present their gifts.

These revenues, along with the empire's mineral deposits, forests, and other natural resources, made the Persian kings wealthy beyond the imagination of the Greeks or Macedonians. For centuries the Persian kings had stored vast treasures in their palaces.

Alexander had virtually the entire Persepolis treasury melted down and recast as coins honoring local kings, beginning with Alexander himself. He set up several mints to make these coins, and minted coins became the standard currency throughout Greece and Persia. This helped unify the empire and put huge amounts of coined money into circulation. It also made many of Alexander's soldiers rich.

Alexander was a generous leader, and he often showed his appreciation for his troops' loyalty by giving them bonuses and lavish gifts. Some of the soldiers began living like kings themselves.

ROYAL ROAD AND TRADE ROUTES

Darius I built many roads that linked the satrapies. The main highway, known as the Royal Road, extended from the Greek city of Ephesus on the Mediterranean coast to the valley of the Indus River. This network of roads enabled the Persians to run an efficient postal service. The Royal Road was divided into 111 post stations, each equipped with fresh horses. The king's messengers changed horses at each station.

The road system helped the Persian kings rule their diverse peoples efficiently. It also enabled them to keep informed of developments throughout their lands. These roads also made it easier for Alexander to conquer the empire. Later, the roads enabled Greek influence to spread more quickly through the Persian Empire.

Macedonian mail riders used the Royal Road, just as the Persians had, to transport mail. Riding horses and special camels bred and trained for speed, they carried mail back and forth between the soldiers in Persia and the Macedonian capital, Pella. The Persian Royal Road was also an important trade route. For centuries, tradesmen had led their caravans (groups of people traveling together, often traders) across dangerous deserts, mountains, and grasslands to sell their goods at market towns. These goods included perfumes, incense, gold, jewelry, pearls, crafts such as silver drinking cups, furs, many types of weapons, horses from Assyria, and cattle from Mesopotamia.

Most trade was local, between villages and the nearest cities. But under Alexander, there was a tremendous increase in trade between east and west. This was due, in part, to the new coins that had been put into circulation and the fact that everyone was using the same currency. It was also helped by the establishment of many new towns and

CONNECTIONS

Neither Snow nor Rain . . .

The Persian road system was extremely efficient. The Greeks were impressed with a practice called *angareion*, which involved riders exchanging horses along the way in a sort of relay race. The Greek historian Herodotus, in his *The Histories*, wrote of this practice, "There is nothing mortal which accomplishes a journey with more speed than these messengers, so skillfully has this been invented by the Persians."

Herodotus's next words are familiar to most people living in the United States: "Neither snow nor rain nor heat nor gloom of night stays these couriers from the swift completion of their appointed rounds." These words are inscribed on the general post office building in New York City and have become the unofficial motto of the United States Post Office.

Traveling Across Time

The long caravan that followed Alexander traveled 11,000 miles back and forth across the Persian Empire. This moving city used the same roads that were later traveled by the Romans, Genghis Khan (ca. 1162–1227 B.C.E.), Marco Polo (1254–1324 B.C.E.), and, later still, by British soldiers during World War II.

Roads that branched out from the Royal Road linked all parts of the empire. One branch connected Babylon and Ecbatana, crossing the Royal Road near Opis and continuing to the Far East. During the first century B.C.E., this route between the Medi-

Part of Alexander's Royal Road eventually became the Silk Road, a key trading route between the East and the West. This medieval painting shows the Italian explorer and trader Marco Polo and his fellow travelers on the Silk Road. Goods, ideas, culture, and technology were carried back and forth along the Silk Road for centuries.

terranean Sea and China became part of what is known as the Silk Road. The first users of this important trade route, which actually included four different roads, probably lived between 1000 and 500 B.C.E.

One of the Silk Road's most famous travelers was Marco Polo, a merchant from Venice, Italy. He first traveled along this route when he was 17 years old. He described the exotic east in a book that remains one of the most famous travel books of all time, *The Travels of Marco Polo*. The book added a great deal to what was known about Asian geography and culture and introduced many Westerners to Asian culture.

New ideas also traveled along the Silk Road. Believers spread both Buddhism and Islam along its route. Technologies such as printing, paper making, ceramic glazing, glass blowing, and wine making were carried between east and west. New foods, such as noodles, which food historians believe originated in Persia, were also introduced to the world via the Silk Road.

Merchants traveled the Silk Road in caravans of camels. Besides silk, which came from China, they used this route to transport many kinds of goods, including gold and silver, rubies and jade, textiles, ivory, spices, furs, ceramics, and bronze weapons. Salt, which for many years was worth as much as gold, was another important Silk Road product.

ports. Another important factor was the adoption of Greek throughout the lands Alexander controlled as the language used for trade and diplomacy. With a single currency and language, commerce was greatly simplified.

For a time, increased economic activity throughout the ancient world relieved some of the economic difficulties that had threatened Greece. Years of fighting among the city-states had caused the farmers (who were required to serve as soldiers in wartime) to neglect their farms, and food became scarce. The economic boom sparked by Alexander's conquests helped temporarily relieve this crisis.

Besides increased trade, war loot also helped. Alexander divided Persian riches among the Greek towns and city-states that had supported the invasion. As one of the leading powers, Athens received a large amount of silver, gold, and luxury items as its share of the war loot.

A new demand arose in the west for goods such as spices that were not produced in the Mediterranean region. Other goods traded between east and west included building materials such as lumber and asphalt, frankincense, myrrh (an aromatic gum resin used to make perfume and incense), gold, metals, gems, grain, horses, oil, pearls, silk, foods, and wine. Wars had created an enormous demand for iron—used for making armor and weapons. Buying and selling slaves was also an important part of trade in Alexander's empire.

Luxury goods were imported from India, Africa, and Arabia. These usually were carried by Bactrian (two-humped) camels, traveling in caravans. Fine

IN THEIR OWN WORDS

Sharing the Persian Wealth

Alexander was generous with the vast wealth of Persia. He shared it with his soldiers and also sent a great deal home to Macedon and Greece. In this section of *Lives*, Greek historian Plutarch describes how much money there was to go around, and how careful Alexander was to make sure everyone got their share.

> After the battle of Issus he sent a contingent to Damascus and seized the Persians' money, baggage, children, and wives. The Thessalian cavalry did particularly well from the booty; they had fought exceptionally well in battle and Alexander sent them on this mission on purpose, because he wanted them to do well out of the booty. But there was more than enough to go round everyone else in the army as well, and after this first taste of gold and silver and women and an eastern way of life, the Macedonians raced like hounds which have found the scent to pursue and track down Persian wealth.

(Source: Plutarch, *Greek Lives*. Translated by Robin Waterfield. New York: Oxford University Press, 1999.)

embroidery, carpets, tapestries, stones, and jeweled vases came from Babylon, where the knowledge of dyes was very advanced. Basic items, such as grain, raw materials, and manufactured goods, were usually shipped by sea through the ports Alexander established. Slaves were also carried in boats. As a result, piracy was a constant problem.

Several regions became prosperous through trade. Phoenicia, located along the Mediterranean Sea in what is modern-day Israel and Lebanon, had many merchants and craftsmen who sold wood, cloth, precious metals, and carvings. The Phoenicians were not a warlike people, but they were expert shipbuilders and sailors. The people of northern Arabia also grew rich this way. They controlled the main travel routes through the Arabian Desert. Persian merchants with caravans of camels used these routes to carry incense from Arabia to other Middle Eastern lands.

Many regions became prosperous as a result of the trade Alexander's armies opened up. Among them were the Phoenicians, who were expert shipbuilders. This carving from about 700 B.C.E. shows a Phoenician ship.

CHAPTER 5

LIVING IN ALEXANDER'S EMPIRE

MORE IS KNOWN ABOUT THE WAY PEOPLE IN GREECE LIVED than about those who lived within the Persian Empire during Alexander the Great's time. Much of what is known about the people who lived in the Persian Empire comes from the Greeks, whose histories were published many years later. The Greeks did not think highly of the Persians, so it is likely that many of their accounts are biased. Distortion of the facts is a common problem whenever history written by the winners in war is the only version available.

Attempts to understand the Persian Empire is further complicated by the fact that it had many diverse peoples, each living according to their own customs. But there were similarities. In both east and west, life was very different for the rich than it was for the poor, and city dwellers had different lifestyles than people who lived in the country.

Greece was not a very fertile region. It was crisscrossed by mountain ranges and only small areas were suitable for farming. Staple crops were cereals. People typically raised goats rather than cows, because goats needed less land for grazing. People also kept sheep, which they used for both wool and meat.

A Greek city-state included the centrally located city and also the villages and small settlements scattered throughout its territory. Life was similar for people who lived in many of the Greek city-states (with the exception of Sparta, a militaristic monarchy where many aspects of life were quite different).

Macedon was a harsh land with many mountains and lowland valleys. It had greater natural resources than Greece, but life was more difficult there. Most Macedonians were poor farmers, and much of

OPPOSITE
Alexander carried Greek culture throughout the lands he conquered. This jar shows people at a symposium. This was an evening drinking party held at someone's home. It was for men only. The symposium could be a wild evening, or it could offer opportunities to socialize, discuss philosophy, and network.

the population lived in small villages and towns. Towns did not have protective walls and were vulnerable to raids by Macedon's northern neighbors, the Thracians.

In most regions of the Persian Empire, most people lived on farms and in small villages. They kept sheep and raised crops such as wheat and barley to make bread, sesame seeds for oil, almonds, and figs. Farm goods were broadly available to the public. Some villages only had a few dozen households. For most villagers, the greatest fear was that an army would arrive and take their young men away, along with most of their food, animals, and supplies. Contact with the government was limited to the tax collector, who came once a year. Life probably did not change very much for most villagers after Alexander took over.

EASTERN MIGRATION

After Alexander the Great conquered the Persian Empire, many Greeks moved to its western regions. They were drawn by the chance to live more prosperous lives than they could at home, where opportunities were limited. A primary reason that Greek culture spread throughout Mesopotamia and the areas to the west was that so many Greeks moved there.

Greeks, as well as people from other cultures, settled in cities such as Alexandria in Egypt and Babylon in Mesopotamia. These Hellenistic cities were centers of trade, science, and the arts. But life was not easy for many of the people who lived in them. There were large gaps between the lifestyles of the rich and the poor. The wealthy lived in splendor and luxury, but most city dwellers lived in miserable conditions. Riots were common, especially in Alexandria.

Many of the people who lived in these cosmopolitan cities integrated Greek and Macedonian customs, art, literature, and lifestyles into their own native cultures. However, most people who lived in the countryside were untouched by much of this Hellenistic influence.

Greeks also settled in the many towns that Alexander and his successors established throughout the former Persian Empire. Many of the new towns and ports were named after Alexander. They were designed to be centers of administration and trade, as well as strongholds that protected the local inhabitants. They served as outposts to keep the peace and to provide warnings to headquarters in case of local uprisings.

New towns were usually built at the junction of important roads and placed where they could overlook the surrounding area. They were established close enough to existing villages to enable the newcomers to associate with the natives. But they were also far enough apart that the Macedonian and Greek settlers could keep to themselves.

The first new settlers in a town were typically older, wounded, or disabled war veterans and Greek mercenaries. Many of the veterans settled down with their war loot and a piece of land. Some had started families with women they met while on the march. Later, merchants, craftspeople, and others joined them.

These new towns were typically built on the Greek model. They had schools, offices, shops, a temple, a council chamber, and a gymnasium. Such a town might also have a theater, a fountain, and a monument. It would always have a public square, which was the focus of all Greek cities.

LIFE IN THE CITY

The typical Greek city was centered on the open market, or agora. City dwellers generally rose at dawn. After washing and eating breakfast, most men would head for the agora (the men did a lot of the marketing). The agora was divided into sections where people sold fish, meat, produce, wine, flowers, and other goods. Fruit vendors would display their best olives and figs at the tops of their baskets and hide the rotten fruit on the bottom.

The agora was the main place where men socialized, as well. At the agora, men would gather under porches supported by many columns. They exchanged gossip and discussed the issues of the day. They also socialized at barbershops or at blacksmiths' workshops, which were warm even during cold weather.

Small businesses and shops of tradesmen, such as upholsterers, barbers, shoemakers, sculptors, doctors, and moneychangers, were located on the streets coming out of the agora. In one section, horse breeders sold or traded animals. In another, men could hire cooks or day laborers to help in the home or field or drive a chariot. There was also a slave market near the agora.

TRAINING THE CHILDREN

In many Greek city-states, poor children began helping on the farm or in workshops by the age of 10. If they lived in the city, both girls and boys would learn a trade by helping their parents in their daily work. The more fortunate might become apprentices to skilled craftspeople. (An apprentice learns a trade by working with a master at that trade.)

In Persia children under the age of five were taken care of by their mothers and other female relatives. Children did not see their fathers very often before the age of five, because it was thought that it would be too hard on their fathers if the children died. (Throughout the ancient world, many children died at a very young age.)

Starting at five, life was different for girls and boys in the former Persian Empire. Girls stayed home and learned homemaking skills, such as spinning thread and weaving cloth. They did not learn to read and write, but they did learn how to sing and play instruments. For boys, formal teaching began at the age of five. Boys typically received religious education and training in trades and special skills. Trades were passed down from father to son. Wealthy Persians who did not need to learn a trade were taught to ride horses and to use a bow and arrow. Persian aristocrats built huge parks and hunted in them.

All children also received training in traditional and family values. They were taught to emphasize strong family ties, to be concerned about their communities, and to accept the authority of the king. They were also taught to tell the truth. Telling a lie was considered to be a huge disgrace.

MARRIAGE AND FAMILY

In the Persian Empire before Alexander, many customs were driven by the need for a large army to maintain the king's power. Persians were encouraged to marry early and to raise large families. Unmarried adults were looked down upon because people thought they were avoiding their duty. Abortion was considered one of the worst crimes and was punishable by death. To produce more children, men were encouraged to practice polygamy (having more than one wife at the same time).

Parents chose husbands for their daughters when the girls were about 11 or 12 years old and the boys were about 13 or 14. Girls married at 15, the age at which they were considered adults. Boys were also thought of as adults at 15, but they married a few years later. By the time a boy turned 25, he would probably have several wives.

When a couple was married the parents of the bride gave the groom's family a dowry, which was wealth the bride brought to her

---

Alexander's Three Wives

Macedonian and Persian kings practiced polygamy. Alexander married three women, all after leaving Macedon. The first was Roxane in 327 B.C.E. Then, in 324 B.C.E., he married both Parysatis, the daughter of a Persian aristocrat, and Stateira, King Darius III's daughter. All of Alexander's marriages were thought to have been motivated by his desire to gain some political advantage.

Persian kings carried polygamy much further. Some had several wives and as many as several hundred concubines (women who officially lived with the king but were not married to him). They all lived together in their own housing. The part of the palace where they lived was forbidden to all but their servants and the king, and was known as a harem.

marriage. The dowry of a well-to-do girl might include precious metals, household items, land, jewelry, money, servants, or slaves.

It was customary for the bride to move into the home of her husband's family. Marrying close relatives, such as an aunt or even a brother or sister, was considered fortunate in the Persian Empire. One reason for this custom may have been to keep the wealth of the dowry in the family.

In most of Greece, the bride's family also provided a dowry. If she was wealthy, this might include land that provided an income, along with personal possessions. A husband was required to maintain the dowry, which could be inherited by the children. If the couple divorced, the husband would have to return it.

A Greek woman's father or guardian would arrange her marriage while she was still a child. Girls married when they were 14 or 15, and men married at the age of about 30. Unmarried women who were not slaves were rare in ancient Greece. A legal marriage began when the bride went to live in her husband's house. The actual ceremony was the procession to the new house.

When they married, husbands became the legal guardians of their wives. Monogamy (marriage to only one person at a time) was practiced throughout ancient Greece. The nuclear family structure—a husband, wife, and children living together—was typical. At different times, other relatives might move in with a married couple.

Though the scene on this third century B.C.E. vase shows a wedding, the vase itself was actually used at a funeral.

SOLDIERING AS A WAY OF LIFE

Every male Greek citizen was required to serve in either the army or the navy. When they turned 18, Athenian men were trained for two years in military discipline and served as police, prison guards, and on garrison duty. They could be called to fight if a war broke out.

The Greeks were disciplined soldiers and were in great demand as mercenaries. One of the reasons that there were so many Greek mercenaries is that soldiering for hire was one of the few ways many Greek men could make a good living. Most fighting was done by part-time citizen-soldiers in small armies.

With water on three sides, the Greeks also maintained a navy. Poorer citizens could become oarsmen in the fleet. Wealthier Athenians who could afford the equipment, which they had to pay for themselves, joined the army as hoplites, or foot soldiers. The hoplite's equipment included helmet, shield, breastplate, shin-guards, sword, and spear. The armor was made of bronze or iron plates sewn onto pieces of linen or leather. Soldiers wore bronze helmets with guards that also protected their cheeks and noses. On top of the helmets they usually had a crest of feathers or horsehair. They wore wool cloaks for warmth.

In Alexander's time the Athenians elected their generals and admirals. A common soldier in one war might be a general in the next. Armies were made up primarily of infantry. Cavalry did not play a large part, because horses were expensive to maintain and Greece's mountainous lands made them less practical.

Before Alexander's father, Philip II, came to power, the Macedonian army was primarily made up of poor farmers who served as amateur soldiers during part of the year. Philip turned these amateurs into skilled soldiers and created a professional army in Macedon. Under Philip, soldiers trained all year round, making long marches with heavy packs to build their strength. Philip also developed a strong and effective Macedonian cavalry. As in Greece, members of the cavalry had to provide and feed their own horses, making this a position for wealthy men.

Shown in a carving, these Immortals were part of a special guard used by Persia's King Darius III.

The strongest military branch in the Persian Empire was the navy. It included about 400 warships built by men from Phoenicia. Military leadership was limited to Persian aristocrats, but all Persian boys entered the military when they turned 18. Males from ages 15 to 50 could be drafted into the army if they were needed. When they returned, they were expected to marry additional wives and have a lot of children.

ALEXANDER'S ENTOURAGE

When ancient kings went to war, long caravans followed their armies to provide them with food, supplies, and other services. The greatest fear of most villagers was that an army and all its followers would arrive and take their young men away, along with food, animals, and supplies that most villages could not spare. Hostile armies simply took whatever they wanted. "Friendly" armies, too, expected—or required—local people to provide food and other supplies. Sometimes, as Alexander's army did, they would pay for these supplies.

Alexander normally did not allow violence and looting in villages where his army was simply passing through. He rarely took all of a village's resources. But even though he usually bought the supplies he needed, most farmers had practically nothing extra to sell. Even if they received money, it was not of much use to them, since there was nothing to buy in the countryside.

Alexander traveled with an enormous "moving city" that stretched for miles. The size of his army changed during the 11 years he was in the east, but of the tens of thousands of people who traveled with Alexander, only about half were soldiers. The rest were employed exclusively to take care of the needs of the troops and the civilians traveling with them. Organizing and transporting the food, water, and equipment necessary for so many people was an incredible challenge. Alexander's massive entourage included:

Animals: Donkeys and mules carried most of the supplies and bulky goods. Eventually camels were also used. Cattle were brought along for food.

Architects: Alexander founded dozens of fortified towns throughout the Persian Empire and needed architects to help design and build them.

Artists and writers: Alexander was a favorite subject for painters and sculptors. He even had his own personal sculptor. He also had an official historian whose job was to immortalize him by writing about his exploits.

Baggage train: Hundreds of wagons carried siege machinery and other large objects. Wounded soldiers were sometimes carried in these wagons as well. Still, Alexander made only limited use of wheeled transport, because wagons require roads or level tracks, and these were limited in most of the regions in which he traveled. The harnesses available at that time for animals to pull wagons were also primitive and inefficient, and wagons were too slow for an army noted for its speed of movement.

Clerks and grooms: Accountants, administrators, clerks, grooms, and slaves were needed to manage the army's funds and carry out day-to-day routines.

Cooks and mess staff: Feeding the army was a full-time job for the large group of people who planned, prepared, and served the food.

Engineers, technicians, mechanics, and tradespeople: About 4,000 engineers, mechanics, boat and bridge builders, sinkers of wells, blacksmiths, carpenters, tanners (people who make leather), and painters created the equipment and artillery the army used. Experts in forestry and soil composition were needed to estimate the position and course of rivers, bays, and gulfs, and to identify sites for possible harbors. Surveyors mapped the lands the army passed through.

Entertainers and athletes: Whenever the troops stopped, there were games and festivals. Athletes competed and poets, dramatists, musicians, singers, storytellers, dancers, acrobats, jugglers, and actors entertained. Construction workers and set painters built and decorated theaters.

Merchants: The market that followed the army was as large as that of a capital city, with a surprising array of goods for sale. Whenever the caravan stopped, horse traders, jewelers, and other merchants set up little markets to supply the newly wealthy soldiers with things to buy.

Scholars, intellectuals, and philosophers: Lively conversation and learning were as important while traveling as they were at home.

Scientists: Conquering may have been Alexander's number one priority, but collecting knowledge was a close second. Mineralogists, zoologists, botanists, and other scientists collected specimens of plants and animals to study. They made important discoveries about the geography, climate, and geology of the east.

Scouts and spies: Cartography (making maps) and acting as translators were among the duties of scouts and spies.

Soothsayers and diviners: Soothsaying, or reading signs and omens to predict the future, was an important job. Astronomers (more like our present-day astrologers) were also on hand to make predictions and give advice.

Women and children: Women whom soldiers had taken as mates along the way, and their children, often traveled with the army.

FASHION STATEMENTS

Greek people wore simple clothing that they wove from wool or plant fibers. They also made clothing from animal skins. The wealthy wore muslin (a cotton cloth) or linen. Both men and women went barefoot indoors and wore a draped garment called a *chiton*, which fell about their body in folds. A woman's *chiton* reached her ankles, a man's reached his knees. The *chitons* were kept close to the body with two belts. Most *chitons* were short-sleeved or sleeveless.

Until Alexander's time, wealthy Greek men had long hair and beards. In ancient Greece, Rome, and the Middle East, intricately groomed long hair was considered a mark of beauty. Caring for it was a time-consuming task that most often only the rich could afford. Slaves and ordinary people, who did

CONNECTIONS

Beauty Is in the Eye

Today, millions of dollars are spent on eye makeup and other cosmetics for enhancing one's looks. Cosmetics was a booming business in Alexander's time too. Even back then, eye makeup was an essential tool for looking good. But it had a practical aspect too. In the dry desert climates, eye makeup protected the delicate skin around the eyes, kept off flies whose bites could cause inflammations, and sheltered the eyes from the sun's glare—just as modern football players paint black streaks under their eyes for the same reason.

Greek women also spent hours on facials and often went to bed wearing a "beauty mask." A popular recipe was one whose main ingredient was flour. It would then be rinsed off with milk the following morning. Just as today, these remedies were meant to give the skin a fresh, young glow. Like modern women, the ancient ones wanted a smooth canvas on which to apply the many colors of their face paint.

CONNECTIONS

Versatile Olive Oil

The Greeks found an amazing number of uses for olive oil. It was used in medicine to disinfect and heal wounds, to maintain metal, as a lubricant, as soap, in religious rituals, to preserve clothing, and as a lamp fuel. Athletes spread it over their bodies as a protection against chilly weather. The Greeks used about 16 gallons of olive oil a year per person. Only about a quarter of this amount was consumed as food.

Although today both Greece and Italy produce large quantities of this fragrant green oil, Spain leads the world in olive oil production. It is still a practical commodity. Modern cold-pressing techniques allow the oil's flavor, color, and nutritional value to be retained for several months without refrigeration.

Cold-pressing is done in many stages, so that the oil is gradually pressed out. The olive oil that comes from the last pressing, called olive foots or olive residue, is inedible. But even at this final stage the oil, as in ancient times, has many uses. Olive residue is an ingredient in soaps and detergents, textiles and medicines, and of course, in cosmetics.

not have the time or the money that elaborate hairstyles required, commonly wore their hair short.

When Alexander joined the Macedonian army, he cut his shoulder-length hair to the neck because he did not want it to interfere with his armor. He also shaved his beard—legend has it that this was to make sure an enemy could not grab him by the chin in close combat. When he became king he ordered his soldiers to shave their beards as well. From his time onward, most Greek men had short hair and stopped wearing beards.

In the Persian Empire, men's beards grew long. They thought it indecent to show any part of their bodies other than their faces, so their clothes draped from head to toe. Both men and women wore long robes. Wealthy people wore elaborate clothes made of luxurious fabrics, such as imported silk. Wealthy men and women both wore jewelry, including rings, earrings, and bracelets set with precious stones.

The king wore a flowing robe of purple (the traditional color of royalty in ancient times) interwoven with gold threads. He also wore a magnificent crown with precious gems and, frequently, beautiful earrings, chains, and bracelets.

Most Macedonians and Greeks thought Persian clothes were too showy. But when he was not in battle, Alexander often wore Persian clothing himself, especially in the later part of his reign. He wore a long robe, cape, sash, and headband in the royal purple and white.

SIMPLE HOMES

In many Greek city-states, the wealthy, army leaders, government officials, and leading merchants had large, comfortable homes, fine clothing, and the best food. Everyone else lived very simply. (A notable exception was Sparta, where the lifestyle even for the wealthy was very spare and simple.)

Although the Greeks built large public buildings, houses were typically small and cramped together in crooked little streets. They were made of materials that could be found locally, such as rough stone, wood, thatch (straw and reeds), and adobe bricks that were made from earth and straw that was dried in the sun. Many houses were made of clay bricks and had very small windows.

The center of household activity was in the back, in rooms arranged around an open courtyard. The windows faced into the courtyard. (Today many Mediterranean houses are built on a similar plan.) In the courtyard was an altar for sacrifices to the gods and a cistern, or tank, to catch rainwater. Water from public fountains had to be carried into the house with jugs—a task that fell to the women or slaves.

The couch was the most important piece of furniture in the Greek home. Couches were used for sleeping, eating, reading, and writing. Plump cushions enabled people to lie back in comfort while eating. They ate from small, round tables with three legs, which were portable and low enough to be pushed under a couch when they were not being used. Lamps made of baked earth or metal burned olive oil for indoor lighting. A person going out at night would carry a torch or a lantern made of horn.

In the Persian Empire raw building materials included mud brick, stone, and timber. Local builders had access to limestone, but did not have granite or marble. Bitumen or mineral pitch, a black, tarry material unique to the Middle and Near East, was

How Sweet It Is

Although sugar was being used in India probably as early as 800 B.C.E., it took its sweet time traveling west into the Persian Empire and beyond. Initially the ancient Greeks and Romans used sugar primarily as a medicine. But Alexander was probably familiar with its taste in a more pleasant context. The royals and other of the most wealthy Greek and Macedonian families also prized it as a food.

It was only in the 10th century that the use of sugar began to spread more widely into Europe. By then traders from Venice were becoming fabulously rich importing sugar, along with silks and spices such as nutmeg and cloves from the Far East. For hundreds of years, sugar remained a rare treat that only the wealthiest could afford. Finally the exotic sweet reached the New World when Christopher Columbus took sugar cane there on one of his expeditions.

One of the best forms of sugar has its roots in the Arabic culture. The Arabs crystallized sugar as a sweet treat they called *qandi*—from which comes the English word "candy."

used for waterproofing and sealing, as a glue, and as mortar for bricks. Baked bricks were sometimes used to build forts, temples, and expensive private homes for the aristocrats and those who worked for the government.

The homes of the wealthy were large and filled with expensive objects and elaborate furnishings. They often had landscaped courtyards and were surrounded by high walls of stone or brick. Zoroastrianism, the largest religion in the Persian Empire, encouraged people to maintain arbors (shady groves), orchards, and gardens. Gardens with roses, shade trees, and citrus or pistachio trees were common. Many gardens also had ponds and fountains. Some of the kings of the Persian Empire planted and maintained trees in their own gardens.

The houses of poor people were much more modest. A typical house was a rectangular, two-story structure. The house was often divided into separate living quarters, and members of one or more extended families lived under the same roof. They used stairs or ladders, placed both inside and outside the house, to get to the second floor.

Most houses were built of unbaked mud bricks. Some were built on a foundation made of fired bricks (firing hardened the brick) or stone. The roof was made of timber beams, which were covered with three layers of material: reed matting, then a layer of lime, and finally a thick layer of mud. The ground floor was earth, covered by reed matting or swept smooth. The top floor might be covered with wool carpet, animal skins, or felt blankets.

SIMPLE FOOD

Macedonians and Greeks ate simply. Bread was the main part of their diet. It was baked from barley imported into Greece from the Persian Empire. Wealthier people were able to make bread from wheat. A family could buy its bread from small bakery stands or make it at home. Wives or household slaves ground the grain, shaped the dough, and baked the bread in a pottery oven that was heated by charcoal.

Greeks also ate vegetables, olives, fruit, and goat cheese. Fish was a popular food in this coastal nation. Wealthier people ate baked turbot, steamed bass, fried shrimp, and smoked herring, as well as squid, eels, and sardines. Vegetables included beans, cabbage, lentils, lettuce, and peas. On special occasions, roasted sheep might be served. Dishes were

Bedbug Spice

The spice known as coriander, native to Greece, is actually the seeds of the cilantro plant. Its name comes from the Greek word *koris* or bedbug, because the Greeks thought the leaves and the unripe seeds of the plant smelled like bedbugs when they were crushed.

flavored with garlic and onions. The Greeks also used salt, which they took from the sea.

Only the wealthy could afford to eat meat regularly. Most people enjoyed it only occasionally. For some, meat was only available when the state provided it as part of animal sacrifices during religious festivals. It was grilled over coals on a pottery brazier, a dish shaped much like a modern picnic grill that contained burning charcoal.

Meat was easier to come by in Macedon, which had a lot of forests. Wild boar and deer were part of the Macedonian diet. People in Sparta also ate more meat than those in the other Greek city-states.

Everything was washed down with wine, mainly from local vineyards. The wine was usually diluted with water. The Greeks

God or Man?

Greek mythology contains many stories of Zeus having children with human women. Many historians believe Alexander's mother, Olympias, told Alexander since his childhood that Zeus was his real father. When Alexander entered Egypt in 332 B.C.E., he visited Siwa, where there was a famous temple to the god Ammon, the Egyptian counterpart of Zeus. According to legend, the oracle confirmed that the god Ammon/Zeus was his true father.

Many historians dispute this story. One theory is that when Alexander entered the temple, the priest greeted him by saying *"o paidion"* ("my child"), but he mispronounced the words and said *"o pai diôn"* ("son of Zeus").

The secret of Siwa has never been known, because Alexander never told anyone what the oracle said to him. However, after that visit the king often wore two ram's horns—the sacred headdress of Ammon.

Later, Alexander petitioned Athens to ask that they grant him the status of god, which they reluctantly did.

drank both white and red wine. The average Greek household produced much of what it needed to survive, including cheese, bread, vegetables, olives, and wine. They could also buy these staples from local markets. Wine, oil, grain, fruits, and vegetables were kept in large clay jars.

Olives, another staple of the Greek diet, were eaten whole or pressed into olive oil. The Greeks poured olive oil over raw vegetables and bread and used it as an ingredient in sauces. With a climate that was excellent for growing olive trees and grape vines, the Greeks made superb olive oil and wine.

A typical Greek breakfast was made up simply of bread and wine. Many Athenians had a light lunch in the mid-morning, often eating the leftovers from their meal the day before. The agora closed at noon, and men might purchase sausages and pancakes covered with honey from a local vendor for lunch. Most people ate just two meals: breakfast and

The cult of Dionysus (in the center), the Greek god of nature and wine, was popular among the Macedonians.

a late lunch. Dinner in the modern sense—a nighttime meal—was unusual.

The Greeks ate everything other than soup with their hands. Food was cut into bite-sized pieces before it was served. In between courses, people wiped their hands on a piece of dough or bread. They later gave this to the family dog to eat. For dessert, they ate figs, nuts, and sticky pastries, which the Greeks invented.

In the Persian Empire, the typical diet of the lower classes included barley, dates, milk, and cheese. Sesame oil rather than olive oil was the main cooking oil.

Because of their extensive trade with outlying parts of the empire, the people in the Persian Empire had an abundance of wheat, meat, wine, honey, citrus fruits, and dried fish. They imported spices from India and had a much spicier diet than did the Greeks.

Most people in the Persian Empire believed that too much food would make them weak and overweight. They generally ate only one meal a day, but that one meal would often stretch out to take up much of the day.

The ancient Persians also developed techniques for farming and raising animals that have lasted through the centuries. They introduced new crops, including barley, alfalfa, and rice, throughout their empire. They also may have been the first to domesticate chickens.

GREEK GODS

The Greeks and Macedonians worshipped hundreds of gods and goddesses and sacrificed to them. The most important were the 12 great Olympian gods. They were believed to live on Mount Olympus in northern Greece, the region's highest mountain. Different gods presided over different aspects of life. Alexander worshipped and sacrificed to many gods, including Zeus, the king of the gods, and Athena, who had been the patron goddess of the hero Achilles—whom Alexander believed was his ancestor on his mother's side of the family.

In addition to worshipping the Olympians, people in different regions practiced local faiths. These involved worshipping various lesser gods and goddesses, including nymphs (minor nature goddesses, typically pictured as beautiful young women), naiads (nymphs who lived in bodies of fresh water, such as brooks, springs, and fountains), river gods, and demons. The Greeks also worshipped demigods—beings who were half human and half god. One of the most famous of these was another man Alexander believed was his ancestor, Heracles (his Roman name was Hercules).

Indian Wise Men

When Alexander and his troops entered India in March 326 B.C.E., they met people with a variety of faiths. At the time Buddhism was about two centuries old and was spreading throughout India. The Buddha was an Indian prince who lived some time between 560 and 480 B.C.E. Saddened by the suffering of the world, he left his luxurious palace and spent the next six years meditating. He then achieved enlightenment—the truth about the world and about the human condition. He taught that to live an unselfish life is the way to end suffering in the world. Some of Alexander's followers became Buddhists.

Alexander also encountered a group of Brahman sages—wise men who wandered naked without possessions and who were fed by the community. Their religion was Hinduism. Having renounced (given up) all physical pleasures and the life of the flesh, they were detached from the joys and pains of the human condition.

Alexander was highly curious about Brahman beliefs and personally interviewed these sages. They told him that people experience many lifetimes and that human existence is a punishment for previous mistakes. They also introduced him to the concept of nirvana, a mental state that enables people to escape from the never-ending chain of reincarnation, or being born again and again.

When the holy men discovered that Alexander's goal was conquest, they stamped the ground to show him that you can only really possess the ground you stand on. Alexander disagreed, but admired their independence. One of them, Calanus (d. 324 B.C.E.), became Alexander's adviser and returned to Persia with him.

The god Dionysus was popular in Macedon. Dionysus was the son of Zeus and a mortal woman. He was the god of nature and fertility and the giver of wine. Alexander's mother, Olympias, participated in rituals honoring him. She was said to have introduced Alexander into this cult at an early age. Alexander honored Dionysus at frequent drinking celebrations, known as *comuses*, and with dramatic performances.

The rules of behavior were based on what people believed the gods expected. For example, the Greeks believed the gods expected them to provide hospitality to strangers and proper burial for family members. They also believed the gods punished humans for arrogance and violence. When misfortune struck, it was considered a sign that someone had offended one of the gods. Offenses might include forgetting to make a sacrifice, violating the purity of a temple area, or breaking an oath or sworn agreement.

The Greeks believed their gods had human form and were, for the most part, physically perfect. Although they were all-powerful, they had many common human faults. They were capable of jealousy, revenge, pettiness, and vanity.

To please the gods, people made sacrifices and offerings. Sacrifices were also made as thanks to the gods for blessings and to enlist their support. Alexander sacrificed to the gods before every battle as well as at many other times. The ritual of sacrifice was the primary form of contact between people and gods.

While individuals could offer sacrifices in their homes, most sacrifices took place as regularly scheduled events in the community. Each city-state had a patron deity, or supporting god, and its citizens honored that god. Athens, for example, was named after Athena, the goddess of wisdom.

Ritual offerings might include art, money and other valuables, fruits, vegetables, and small cakes. Animal sac-

CONNECTIONS

Gifts of the Magi

The leaders of Zoroastrianism were priests, or wise men, called *magi*. By the first century C.E. the word in its singular form—*magus* or *magos*—was often in use to mean a mysterious person who had access to secret knowledge that was not available to the common people. It is used this way in the Bible. From these roots came the English word *magic*.

The most famous magi were the three wise men who visited Jesus Christ when he was born. A star is said to have led them to his location in a manger in Bethlehem. They brought him gifts of gold, frankincense, and myrrh—goods that were commonly traded between east and west.

The symbol on the wall is part of Zoroastrianism, the dominant religion of the Persian Empire.

rifice was a tradition that may have come from prehistoric hunters who wanted to show respect for the divine forces that provided them with animals for food. Animal sacrifice involved strict rules and elaborate procedures. Different cults had different rituals, all performed by priests and priestesses. One of the few rights Greek women had was that of becoming priestesses.

Every Greek temple was dedicated to a particular god. These structures were looked upon as places where the gods and goddesses they were built for actually lived. Temples were typically rectangular and made of marble. Inside stood brightly painted marble statues of the particular god or goddess, with an altar in front.

Some temples had special shrines known as oracles, at which the gods were believed to communicate with human beings. These communications, including answers to questions and interpretation of signs, came through a priest or priestess at the shrine, who was also called an oracle. Often the answers these oracles provided were not very clear and could have more than one meaning.

The Macedonians were very tolerant of other religions. For centuries they had incorporated the beliefs and gods of other religions into their own. Alexander offered sacrifices to the local gods in the areas he conquered.

RELIGION IN THE PERSIAN EMPIRE

The kings of the Persian Empire allowed people in the nations they defeated to practice their own customs and follow their own religious beliefs. However, most people in the Persian Empire, along with the kings, followed Zoroastrianism. Its founder was a prophet named Zoroaster, whom historians believe to have lived some time between 1000 and 600 B.C.E. in what is now Uzbekistan. (A prophet is a person who is considered to be an inspired teacher or someone who declares the message of God.)

The Zoroastrians believe there is one supreme god, Ahura-Mazda. He created everything that was good, including heaven, earth, people, truth, joy, light, and fire. But Ahura-Mazda had an evil twin brother, known simply as the Evil One, who created everything bad.

In contrast to the Greeks, who believed that people's lives were controlled by the gods, the Persians believed they could choose between good or evil. Zoroaster preached that the world was the arena for a constant battle between good and evil. Every time someone did or thought something good, he or she was strengthening the power of Ahura-Mazda. Whenever people behaved badly, they were tipping the balance in favor of the Evil One.

IN THEIR OWN WORDS

Praise Good Thoughts

The Avesta is the scared text of Zoroastrianism. It is usually divided into sections relating to ritual, hymns of praise, the liturgy (religious service), and the law. Yasna is the main book of liturgy, or worship. It is also the word used for the Zoroastrian act of worship. This text is from the Yasna introduction, verse four.

I praise good thoughts, good words, and good deeds and those that are to be thought, spoken, and done. I do accept all good thoughts, good words, and good deeds. I do renounce all evil thoughts, evil words, and evil deeds.

(Source: "Yasna (sacred liturgy) Avesta." Zoroastrian Archives. Available online. URL: http://www.avesta.org/yasna/y0to8s.htm. Accessed May 5, 2008.)

CONNECTIONS

Zoroastrianism Today

Zoroaster's teachings spread to nearby lands during the Hellenistic period, and influenced the development of other religions. For example, the Persians believed that Ahura-Mazda appointed a guardian angel for every person on earth. The concept of angels was later absorbed into the beliefs of Judaism and Christianity, along with other aspects of Zoroastrianism, such as a final judgment day.

Zoroastrian teachings have been passed down orally for centuries. Its followers still perform ancient rituals, such lighting lamps and tending sacred trees. Fire still plays a central role, and Zoroastrian sanctuaries are called fire temples.

In Iran today, Islam has largely replaced Zoroastrianism. But a few thousand Zoroastrians still practice their ancient religion there. The largest population of Iranian Zoroastrians can be found in the desert town of Yazd, which dates back to the Sassanian times (224–651). Local Zoroastrians claim that the sacred fire housed inside Yazd's *ateshkadeh*, or fire temple, has been burning since the fourth century C.E.

Outside of Iran, the largest population following this religion today can be found in Bombay, India. Its members are descended from Persians who moved there more than 1,000 years ago. There is also a sizeable Zoroastrian population in Los Angeles.

Zoroaster discouraged animal sacrifice. He preached that animals were too valuable to kill. Fire was an important part of Zoroastrian religious rituals, and many trees are considered to be sacred.

Unlike the Greeks, the peoples of the Persian Empire did not depict their gods as human beings. Stone carvings portrayed Ahura-Mazda as a winged god who often appeared to be blessing the kings. Although people believed the Persian kings were superior to other humans, they were not considered gods but rather the agents of Ahura-Mazda.

Some people in the Persian Empire also worshipped other gods. For example, a popular religious festival in ancient Persia was held in honor of Mithra, the sun god.

CHAPTER 6

ART, SCIENCE, AND CULTURE ACROSS THE EMPIRE

AFTER ALEXANDER CONQUERED THE PERSIAN EMPIRE, Greek became the official language of government, education, and international trade, but native languages continued to be spoken. This was especially true in Egypt, where Greek was hardly spoken outside of Alexandria. But all important discussions and documents were in Greek.

A universal language enabled an unprecedented exchange of ideas. Education in the Greek language extended knowledge of Greek culture. Because of their high regard for knowledge and learning, the Greeks had many documents and books translated into Greek. As a result, the Greeks and Macedonians became increasingly aware of the achievements of other civilizations. As eastern knowledge became more accessible to the west, new understanding began to challenge the old distinction between "civilized" Greeks and "barbarians."

GREEK IDEALS OF EDUCATION

The Greeks highly valued learning and education. In some ways, this was the basis for the power and lasting influence of the culture in which Alexander was raised, and which he spread. Under Alexander, and during the Hellenistic period after he died, education became more

OPPOSITE

A leaping ram decorates this bronze oil lamp, found in Shabwah in modern-day Yemen. Its elegant style is Hellenistic.

This small figure is of a teacher, an important person in Greek and Macedonian society. Children of the aristocracy had a thorough education in philosophy, military science, and the arts, plus military and physical training.

widespread in both Greece and the former Persian Empire. But in both societies it was still available exclusively to the wealthy and, for the most part, only to boys.

Among the poor, the level of literacy in Greece was very low. Most poor people could do little more than sign their names. It was easy, however, for most people to find someone who could read to them if they needed to understand a written text, such as a letter. Most communication was therefore oral rather than written. This meant most people were able to absorb a lot of information by ear.

Both rich and poor Greeks liked songs, speeches, and stories, and memorized many of them. In Persia, too, most people were illiterate and recited stories and poems from memory.

In contrast, male children of wealthy Greek parents were highly educated. That education was aimed at developing the complete individual. The Greeks had little respect for specialists, not even great athletes or philosophers. Their ideal man was someone who was both a philosopher and an athlete, who could take part intelligently in public affairs and also wrestle well. He would also have to be a witty guest at a party or banquet, since lively conversation was highly valued.

The Greeks believed that a healthy body was necessary for a good mind. Boys attended different schools for mental and physical training. Wealthier families might hire a private tutor or have a household slave, called a pedagogue, teach children at home.

Greek boys from well-to-do families started going to school when they were seven years old. Until the age of 14, they focused on reading, writing, numbers, and music. They learned to read by studying Homer's two great works, the *Iliad* and the *Odyssey*. To practice writing, they used a sharp wooden stick called a stylus. They wrote on a waxed wooden block that could be scraped clean and used again and again. When the wax wore down to the wood, they simply applied more wax. Boys learned numbers using pebbles and an abacus, or counting board. Students who misbehaved in class were struck with a rod.

In music school, boys learned to play pipes as well as the flute and the lyre, a stringed instrument with a sound box made from the shell of a tortoise. The strings were plucked with a disk called a plectrum (a word still used in English). Music was played at almost every Greek social event.

When boys reached the age of 14, other subjects were added to their studies. These included geometry, literature, astronomy, drawing, rhetoric (the art of persuasive speaking), and sports. Sports took place in a gymnasium, where boys exercised naked. The main sport was wrestling. The goal of a wrestling match was to force the opponent's shoulders to the ground three times. Boys were also taught to dance.

Higher education began in the fourth century B.C.E. in Athens, at the academy founded by the philosopher Plato (427–347 B.C.E.). Schools of philosophy were available for men over 18. These provided what would today be considered a college education. The leading

The Art of Rhetoric

Rhetoric and oratory were important aspects of a Greek education. Oratory is the art of speaking well in public. Rhetoric is the skill of putting together arguments that inspire and persuade. A person might have one skill and lack the other. The truly accomplished person, such as Alexander, had both. His career is marked by a series of rousing speeches that inspired his soldiers when the odds were against them.

philosopher of the school would deliver lectures, conduct panel discussions, and pose complex questions to the students.

ALEXANDER'S EDUCATION

Alexander was a Macedonian prince being prepared for the throne, so he received a first-rate education. But he did not always enjoy his educational experiences. His first tutor was a man named Leonidas (dates unknown). The stern Leonidas toughened Alexander physically. Leonidas required Alexander to engage in physical exercise before dawn, sometimes forcing him to march for hours before breakfast to increase his appetite. Leonidas insisted on a lean, simple diet and believed being hungry was good discipline. He would search Alexander's belongings to make sure his mother, Olympias, had not snuck him any treats.

Leonidas taught Alexander skills such as running, memorizing lessons, riding a horse, driving a chariot, and using a sword and a spear. Historians have credited Alexander's later ability to endure the many extreme hardships of his war campaigns to the tough discipline he was subjected to under Leonidas.

When Alexander was 13, his father hired Plato's student, Aristotle, to replace Leonidas. With this great teacher Alexander studied literature, philosophy, ethics (the moral principles of behavior), geography, zoology, botany, scientific criticism, drama, poetry, art, law, and politics. Both physical and spiritual qualities were emphasized in the young prince's education.

He learned to sing and play a lyre and received training in physical fitness and warfare. Aristotle also instilled in his young student a lifelong love of the writings of Homer. Alexander believed in the ideal Homer expressed, that honor and glory were achieved through personal success. He tried to be like the heroes Heracles and Achilles in Homer's stories.

Alexander had a great respect for learning, and during his years in the Middle East he often ordered books to be sent to him from Greece. He also sent Aristotle a great deal of money over the years to fund his research and educational projects.

In some cases, the king also looked after the education of his soldiers' children. As the army moved from place to place, many soldiers left behind children who were half Persian and half Greek or Macedonian. Alexander placed many of these children under state protection

More than Enough

When Alexander was a boy, his tutor, Leonidas, criticized him for using too much incense when performing a sacrifice to the gods. He threw two fistfuls of incense on the altar fire and Leonidas told him not to waste such valuable goods. When Alexander captured Gaza, the spice center for the Middle East, he sent Leonidas a gift of 18 tons of incense. He also sent a note to his former tutor urging him not to be stingy toward the gods.

and arranged for their education. They were given military instruction and also learned about the ideals of Greek culture.

MEDICINE IN ALEXANDER'S TIME

Medicine in ancient Greece dates back thousands of years. But the first real hospitals there came into being, according to historians, in the fourth century B.C.E. This was around the time of Alexander. Greek knowledge and techniques of health and healing were already so well-known and respected by then that Romans often employed Greek physicians rather that Roman ones (who were usually slaves). Ancient Greek writings indicate that even the peoples of the Persian Empire preferred Greek, and sometimes Egyptian, doctors.

In Alexander's day, herbs had become an important part of the healing arts. Myrrh, frankincense, and many other herbs were used to treat disease, though no one really understood why they worked. Garlic was used as a remedy for, among other things, breathing problems, parasites, and insomnia. Baths were important for purification of body and soul.

Also in Alexander's time, healing cults (religious groups) were common. There were many active healing temples throughout Greece. One of the most common practices in these temples was incubation—a technique of healing that involved sleeping through the night wrapped in a white sheet and hoping for remedies or cures to be provided in dreams. Ill patients came from all over in hopes of being healed through incubation. There are ancient records of many apparently miraculous cures, after which the happy patient would leave some form of payment at the temple. The poorest left whatever they could—a lock of hair, their shoes—or they simply sang a song of gratitude. Wealthier patients paid accordingly.

EASTERN AND WESTERN SCIENCE

Science blossomed during the Hellenistic period. Because of the increase in the exchange of ideas between East and West, rapid progress was made in a number of fields. These included philosophy, medicine, and mathematics. Greek and Babylonian scholars collaborated in the areas of mathematics, science, and astronomy. Technology also advanced, and many new machines and instruments were invented.

As in other areas, much more is known about Greek science than about science in the Persian Empire. One reason is that an impressive

Time for a Bath

Hot baths first became widespread in Greece in the fourth century B.C.E., so they would have been a luxury Alexander enjoyed. Greek men sometimes took several baths a day.

Most baths were in public bathhouses, but the wealthy also had bathing facilities at home. Attendants helped bathers by pouring water over their bodies. The bath was not only a means of washing. It was a kind of divine purification, a spiritual event. It was thought to renew the soul.

Baths were also considered necessary for the health of the human body. A complete body bath was prescribed for healing hysteria. Soaking the head in cold water was prescribed for a hemorrhage, or massive bleeding. Sponge baths were a way to calm and relax. Such healing baths had very specific rules and required skilled assistants, a room with fresh air, and specific sacrifices.

Greek collection of literary, scientific, and other texts still exists. Documents predating Alexander's conquests in the Persian Empire have not fared as well.

This is partly because paper made from papyrus became more commonly used. But papyrus was hard to preserve in climates other than that of Egypt. Therefore, beyond several relatively short public inscriptions, there is little written documentation of the period between the fall of Nineveh in Assyria in 612 B.C.E. and Alexander's invasion. This fact has long frustrated scholars and historians.

Public bathhouses, offering hot baths, were widespread in Greece. These remains of such a bathing place are in Nemea, Greece. Alexander himself often took several baths a day.

One thing that *is* clear is that the scientific perspectives of Greece and the Middle East were somewhat different. The Greeks believed everything could be understood through science, that knowledge was based on reason, and that all the natural sciences rested on a foundation of mathematics and geometry. They believed one mastered a subject through the method of inquiry. Sometimes this kind of inquiry even challenged the Greeks' traditional religious beliefs.

The Greeks were the first to develop many fields of science. Scientists included practitioners of philosophy, geometry, physics, economics, mathematics, chemistry, biology, psychology, and other fields.

In the Persian Empire people also studied, explored, and experimented. But their science took a more practical turn. Their emphasis was not on understanding the nature of the world through science, since religion already explained the nature of the world. Instead, they wanted to learn how to adapt to the forces that affected the world. In fact, the Persians made many contributions to the world of science. Their practical advances included windmills and water management systems.

ANCIENT STAR GAZING

The city of Babylon, in central Mesopotamia, was a center of science and mathematics. Babylonian mathematicians made great advances in geometry and were among the greatest astronomers in the world.

They calculated the distance of the sun and the moon from the earth with great precision. They understood scientific facts that would not be widely known elsewhere until Italian astronomer Galileo Galilei's (1564–1642) discoveries in the early 17th century. They knew, for example, that the earth turned on its axis, that planets revolve around the sun, and that the sun is much larger than the earth.

Each night for centuries, Babylonian astronomers and priests climbed to the tops of tall towers to observe the moon and stars and record their movements. They kept track of celestial events (things they observed in the sky) such as the exact times the sun and moon rose and set.

One of the discoveries Alexander's men made in Babylon was the astronomical diary of the temple of Marduk, the most important Babylonian god. The officials of this temple had systematically described their celestial observations. One of them, Kidinnu (ca. 4th century B.C.E.), was the first to accurately estimate the length of the year. He calculated that a year was 365 days, 5 hours, 44 minutes, 12.52 seconds (instead of 48 minutes, 45.17 seconds, which was generally accepted at the time). He also proposed a reform of the calendar based on these findings.

When the reports of the Babylonian astronomers were translated into Greek, this new knowledge was immediately applied. The Greek astronomer Callippus (ca. 370–ca. 300 B.C.E.) recalculated the length of a month and came up with a new calendar that had a slightly longer cycle than the one the Greeks had previously used. His new era began on June 28, 330 B.C.E.—only eight months after Alexander captured Babylon.

Middle Eastern astronomers also discovered that there were two days each year, one in the spring and one in the fall, when night and day are of equal lengths. These days are now called equinoxes, which means "equal nights."

READING THE SIGNS

Personal horoscopes were first developed in Babylon about 50 years before Alexander was born. A horoscope is a chart based on the position of the sun, moon, and planets at the time of a baby's birth. The ancient astronomers believed that people's personalities and actions were determined or influenced by the position of these celestial bodies when they were born.

It was common for ancient people to make important decisions based on their horoscopes. Many people throughout the world still

Father of Botany

The philosopher Theophrastus (ca. 372–ca. 287 B.C.E.) is sometimes called the father of botany, which is the study of plants. He gave botany its start by writing detailed books about plant life, such as his *Historia Plantarum*. Much of the information in Theophrastus's writings was said to have been gathered by Alexander during his eastern campaigns.

believe in this practice, known as astrology. In Alexander's time, astrology was thought of as a science.

Astrology was one of many ways ancient people believed they could divine, or predict, the future. Another form of divination involved birds. Bird observers were common in Asia Minor, and predicted the future based on the behavior of birds.

In Greece, predicting the future was also considered an important scientific pursuit. Divination involved various methods of understanding what the gods were communicating to humans. Ancient Greeks used dreams to make predictions and to provide clues as to what humans might have done to anger the gods. They depended on soothsayers, also known as seers, divinators, or prophets, to interpret signs and omens. The Greeks widely trusted these soothsayers to accurately understand and interpret omens such as the weather, the flight of birds, and other phenomena that they believed revealed what the gods were thinking or planning.

One of Alexander's most valued advisors was the soothsayer Aristander. Whenever something important was planned, or any time something strange happened or a new phenomenon was encountered, Aristander's job was to interpret its meaning.

Before battles, Alexander sacrificed animals to the gods to enlist their support for the Macedonians. Marks on the animal's entrails (internal organs) were believed to be omens that indicated how the battle would turn out. Special hooks were used to pull the flesh back from the organs so the marks could be revealed.

Before the decisive Battle of Gaugamela, for example, Aristander predicted victory based on his examination of the entrails of a ram that had been sacrificed. This sign agreed with another omen—an eclipse of the moon that occurred shortly before the battle—which Aristander had interpreted to mean that the Macedonians would win at Gaugamela.

Military strategies were sometimes based on the interpretation of omens. When an eagle landed on a rock near ships on the Phoenician coast, Aristander saw this as an omen that Alexander should look for victory on land instead of at sea. This proved to be a successful strategy.

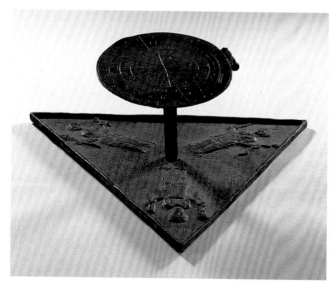

Like an ancient Ouija board, this metal instrument was used by prophets and seers to predict the future.

Signs and Omens

One of the most famous predictions about Alexander concerns the founding of Alexandria in Egypt. Alexander poured peeled grains of barley to mark out a plan for streets and the spots where he wanted certain buildings to be placed. Birds ate the barley. At first Alexander saw this as a bad omen. However, his soothsayer, Aristander, said it meant the city would attract a great number of settlers and that they would all be provided with what they needed to live.

Omens could also be interpreted after something happened. After Alexander's drunken murder of his friend Cleitus, soothsayers found omens that they believed had predicted this terrible event. For one, when Cleitus entered the banquet hall, some sheep followed him in. This was later interpreted as a sign that the gods had intended him to become a sacrifice.

In the spring of 328 B.C.E., soldiers discovered two springs bubbling out of the ground by the side of the Oxus River, where the army had set up camp. One was water, the other was a liquid that the soldiers compared to olive oil. No one realized at the time that it was petroleum—the oily, flammable substance used today in making gasoline and other products. When Aristander was called on to interpret this omen, he said the spring was a sign that there would be hard labors ahead, followed by victory.

Throughout Alexander's campaigns, favorable omens gave him confidence that the gods were blessing his actions. But not all omens were encouraging. Some accounts of Alexander's final entrance into Babylon in 323 B.C.E. mention that a large number of ravens filled the skies. The birds were pecking each other and some fell dead at the feet of the returning king. Soothsayers believed this to be a bad omen and advised him not to enter the city. Astronomers cautioned him that the stars also foretold trouble if he went ahead. Alexander did not follow their warnings. Instead, he marched triumphantly into the city. A few months later, he died in Babylon.

ANCIENT TECHNOLOGIES

It is difficult to determine what Greek technologies Alexander may have introduced into the east. But during his time many practical methods of gathering information and making life simpler were in use.

IN THEIR OWN WORDS

A Good Omen

In an age when generals and commanders were mostly aristocrats who had very little contact with their soldiers, Alexander was an exception. He treated his soldiers well and they followed him with absolute loyalty. This story from Plutarch shows how good-natured Alexander was with his army. It also shows how quickly a light-hearted game could become an omen (a sign of what will happen in the future) for Alexander and his men.

After he had reduced all Asia on this side of the Euphrates, he advanced towards Darius, who was coming down against him with a million of men. In his march a very ridiculous passage happened. The servants who followed the camp for sport's sake divided themselves into two parties, and named the commander of one of them Alexander, and the other Darius. At first they only pelted one another with clods of earth, but presently took to their fists, and at last, heated with contention, they fought in good earnest with stones and clubs. . . . Till Alexander, upon hearing of it, ordered the two captains to decide the quarrel by single combat, and himself armed him who bore his name, while Philotas did the same to him who represented Darius. The whole army were spectators of this encounter, willing from the event of it to derive an omen of their own future success. After they had fought stoutly a pretty long while, at last he who was called Alexander had the better, and for a reward of his prowess had 12 villages given him. . . .

(Source: Plutarch, *Alexander*. Translated by John Dryden. "The Internet Classics Archive." Available online. URL: http://classics.mit.edu/Plutarch/alexandr.html. Accessed June 10, 2008.)

Mapmaking was one of these. At a time when few people knew much about the world beyond their own town or farm, mapmaking, though difficult, was a crucial activity. One method used by the mapmakers who traveled with Alexander was to count and record the number of steps they took each day walking from one camp to the next. Their footstep counts were used as the basis for the maps they created.

The science of metrology (the theory and investigation of making measurements) in Alexander's time is not well documented. One thing that is known is that Alexander's conquests had a significant impact on the development of this science in the lands he controlled. These regions widely adopted the Greek metrological systems. The widespread minting of coins under Alexander's rule made it practical to give the various coins names for the first time. The names corresponded to their set value, making it easier to standardize the relative value of goods.

The peoples of the former Persian Empire made innovations of their own during this time. They developed a very clever method of sending royal orders across their vast empire. Between Susa and Persepolis, they placed high lookout posts close enough for a shout to be heard between them. The local inhabitants with the loudest voices were stationed at these posts as guards. A guard would pass along an order by shouting it across to the next guard, who would do the same until the message had been delivered. In this way, an order traveling the distance of a 30-day journey by foot would be received on the same day.

Another essential technology helped move water from one place to another. Because of the arid (very dry) climate in which they lived, the people in the Middle East had a great respect for water. They developed a system for transporting water throughout their empire known as *qanats*. *Qanats* were underground channels that carried water from the foothills of the mountains in the north to remote, dry areas, such as the plains regions of the south. This irrigation system linked many wells along its route.

The *qanat* tunnels reached down and into the water table—the level below ground where water always flows. Other shafts provided ventilation and access for cleaning and repairing the tunnels. This technology spread because of a policy King Darius I had introduced. As an incentive to people to spend the time and money to build *qanats*, he declared that anyone who brought water to arid areas would be allowed to cultivate the land for five generations.

> **Floating Bridges**
>
> Alexander's soldiers built floating bridges across Indian rivers. They did this by tying boats together and putting planks of wood on top of them. They could then float supplies and horses across the river. This method of building bridges is still used in the Punjab.

HELLENISTIC ART

The arts also flourished in the Hellenistic world, especially painting, sculpture, crafts, and architecture. Greek designs became more complicated as a result of the influence of ideas and techniques from other lands. Similarly, artists in Asia and the Middle East adopted elements of the Greek style. The mingling of these two approaches evolved into a new style of art that incorporated both Greek and Asian ideas.

This new style became known as Hellenistic art. It emphasized showing things in a more natural and realistic way than had previously been popular. This was especially true of the way the human body was depicted.

Hellenistic art also reflected a move away from religious themes. Artists focused on more intense human emotions and portrayals that tried to

CONNECTIONS

Darius Was Here

Persia's system of *qanats*, introduced in about 500 B.C.E., was crucial for carrying water to remote places of that arid empire. As recently as 1933, all of the city of Tehran's water came from this underground irrigation system. One *qanat* linked the Nile River to the Red Sea. Along the length of this great *qanat*, which was 87 miles long and 164 feet wide, were a number of monuments.

In the 1860s, when workers were digging the Suez Canal (which connects the Mediterranean Sea with the Red Sea), they found fragments of a red granite monument marking Darius's *qanat*. At one time, this monument had stood about 9.8 feet tall and 8.2 feet wide. It had an inscription written in four languages: Old Persian, Babylonian, Elamite (the language of Elam, an ancient kingdom in today's southwestern Iran), and Egyptian.

The words, from Darius I (quoted in A. T. Olmstead's *History of the Persian Empire*), read, "I am a Persian. From Parsa I seized Egypt. I commanded this canal to be dug from the river, Nile by name, which flows in Egypt, to the sea which goes From Parsa. Afterward this canal was dug as I commanded, and ships passed from Egypt through this canal to Parsa as was my command."

show the inner character of their subjects. Often Hellenistic art also features more dramatic poses and high contrasts between light and shadow.

Greek artists first began to portray the human form in this new way during the fifth century B.C.E. During the classical age of Greece (approximately 500 to 400 B.C.E.), sculptors and other artists experimented with new techniques and approaches. While the paintings and sculptures of earlier civilizations were often stiff and not lifelike, the Greeks became the first to show realistic human forms in their art. Though no Greek paintings have survived, much sculpture remains. Most of it is made of marble or bronze.

The influence of Hellenistic art can be traced all along Alexander's path, from the Hindu Kush Mountains to the mouth of the Indus River. Archaeologists have discovered many buildings and statues on the border of India and Persia that show the influence of Hellenistic art. These works are much more naturalistic and complex than the art that was done before Alexander.

In the region of Gandhara in India (today's Afghanistan and Pakistan), which Alexander invaded in 326 B.C.E., a new style of art was developed. It combined Buddhist thought with Greek artistic concepts. The Gandhara style played an important role in the development of

Indian art. For example, many statues of the Buddha were modeled after the Greek god Apollo. Even in Turkestan and China—countries Alexander never visited—the Buddha statues are influenced by the Hellenistic sculptural style. Early Christian art was Hellenistic as well.

As Alexander marched through many different regions, he had skilled craftsmen traveling with his army. This enabled artists and craftsmen from many regions to share their skills, or at least see each other's work. Greek craftsmen, who were considered among the best in the world, were influenced by Persian crafts. For example, they became familiar with the Persian rhyton, an ornate drinking vessel often made in the shape of

The Tripylon (triple gate) stairway at Persepolis was added in the sixth or fifth century B.C.E. It is about 22 feet wide and has beautiful stonework reliefs along the sides. This part shows Persian courtiers.

an animal's head. After the war, large quantities of such rhytons appeared in Athens. Greek artists immediately began imitating them.

ARCHITECTURE

Perhaps nowhere was the Greek influence more obvious than in city planning and architecture. This was certainly true in the new towns that Alexander founded. But it was also so in existing cities. Just about everywhere that Alexander's conquests took him, Greek and Macedonian soldiers settled. Some—those injured or too old—were regularly left behind as the troops pressed onward. Others, once their army service was done, returned to places within the new kingdom that they had marched through or fought in before.

When they settled, they brought with them the Greek vision of what a good city should be. The locations of streets and buildings were planned according to Greek standards. The design of new buildings was based on Greek ideals of architecture.

According to the Greek model, public structures were needed for political, economic, and recreational activities. As Alexander conquered and founded cities and his soldiers settled in them, huge building projects became commonplace. Government facilities, public meeting houses, courts of law, and gymnasia sprung up. So did Macedonian-style palaces and the religious and military facilities that were an equally important part of everyday life. Greek style homes filled with Greek household items and decorations could be seen everywhere.

The Macedonians also built stadiums, hippodromes (oval stadiums for chariot races), theaters, and amphitheaters. They created streets lined with columns and public baths. These structures lasted until the Arab invasions in the 600s C.E. Even then, two Greek features—the agora, or marketplace, and the *balaneia* or *thermae*, the baths—become an important part of Islamic architecture as well.

PERSIAN DESIGN

Persian design was more colorful, grand, and elaborate than that of Greece. The kings of the Persian Empire built magnificent palaces and decorated them lavishly. The stairway of King Darius's palace at Persepolis was carved with portraits of people from many different parts of his empire. The vast royal hall, supported by many dozens of carved stone columns, could hold 10,000 people. Artisans from across the

Seven Wonders of the Ancient World

The Seven Wonders of the Ancient World were the major landmarks of the Hellenistic world. The list was a kind of "must-see" for Greek tourists, and was compiled by various Greek historians. As a result, their list is limited to sights around the Mediterranean.

The first three were the statue of Zeus in Olympia, the Great Pyramids in Egypt, and the Hanging Gardens of Babylon. These three sites form a triangle that identifies the economic heartland of Hellenistic civilization.

The other four wonders were the Temple of Artemis in Ephesos, the Mausoleum of Mausolus in Halicarnassus, the Colossus of Rhodes, and the Pharos, or lighthouse, of Alexandria. Of all these wonders, only the Great Pyramids remain today.

empire carved numerous stone monuments in Persepolis and other royal capitals.

Stone carvings often portrayed the kings' pride in their military conquests. Monuments carved on cliffs depicted great military achievements. They showed victorious leaders and defeated enemies.

Unlike Persepolis, Susa was not close to sources of stone. Materials had to be brought in from throughout the empire to build the royal palace at Susa. These included wood, gold, silver, ebony, and ivory.

The palace incorporated

CONNECTIONS

Roses from the Angels

The Persians loved farming and gardening. They enjoyed all flowers, especially those with rich, heavy fragrances. And they prized the rose above all others. Sacred ancient Persian texts speak of roses as first being grown by angels.

The Rose of Damascus, one of the most fragrant species, is a flower with a long history. It first grew wild in the Middle East. Gardeners often transplanted it from the wilds into their gardens, along with other wild flowers.

This exotic rose eventually found its way to Spain and France. It became known in Britain during the time of Henry VIII (1491–1547). In the western world, the rose of Damascus became known as the much-loved Damask rose.

styles and techniques from stonecutters, goldsmiths, woodworkers, and glazed-brick makers from all over the empire. It was decorated with pictures of men, monsters, and gods made from tiles and glazed bricks. The clay bricks were coated with colorful glazes made of crushed rocks, salt, and powdered clay. They were then baked in a kiln (a large, very hot oven) to create a thin, shiny surface.

Babylon was a spectacular city with a huge temple and a grand royal palace. The road leading to the temple was decorated with lions, flowers, and patterns made of glazed bricks. The palace's hanging gardens were famous and were considered one of the Seven Wonders of the Ancient World.

From the wealth of materials that came into their lands, the people of the Persian Empire created all kinds of beautiful works. They made fine jewelry out of silver and carpets out of wool. These intricately designed carpets were highly valued and are still very expensive and rare today. Persian aristocrats decorated their homes with beautiful sculptures, delicate vases, and luxurious fabrics. Their homes, like the palaces, were designed to command respect.

In contrast to the Persians, Greek architecture was typically very regular and rectangular in shape during Alexander's time. But a number of round buildings were constructed as well. These exceptions, which include *tholoi*—circular buildings with pointed or domed roofs—are considered by some to be a result of the Persian influence on Greek architecture.

There was another important result of this fusion of west and east. The great stores of wealth that Alexander claimed in the Persian Empire had a direct and striking effect on architecture and building in Greece.

Before Alexander's time, even traditional Greek buildings such as gymnasia and theaters had been relatively plain. With the riches that Alexander and his army sent home, such buildings became monumental complexes. The sometimes awe-inspiring appearance of Greek architecture that today we take for granted could not have been possible without Alexander's eastern expansion.

RECREATION AND LEISURE

The Greeks gave as much importance to buildings for entertainment and leisure activities as they did their architecture for business and political purposes. Alexander, like most Greeks, was a great fan of entertainment of all kinds.

Among the favorite activities of Greek men were good conversation, athletics, and politics. In the afternoon, men would attend a lecture, exercise at a gymnasium, or bathe in a public bathhouse. Relaxing at the public baths was a primary form of recreation. Some of the baths contained gambling rooms. There, men would throw dice or play a game called knucklebones, or five-stones, which was similar to jacks.

Dinner parties were also a favorite leisure activity of the Macedonians and the Greeks. Following dinner, wealthy men often held a symposium, or drinking party. At these all-male festivities, guests would have intellectual discussions about political or scientific topics, taking turns to speak. They would also pose riddles to one another. A guest who was unable to solve the riddle might have to drink a glass of salted wine as punishment. Acrobats, singers, musicians, and dancers entertained at these gatherings. There were few events that did not include music.

Younger Greeks had their own forms of amusement. Like their elders, teenagers played knucklebones, a game similar to dice that is still popular in some places today. Players throw and catch five small objects (originally sheep's knucklebones) in different ways. Teens also played with balls and tops. They played hopscotch and a game that is similar to marbles but used nuts instead.

Board games were another popular entertainment, mostly among adults. Many of these boards featured a circular path that had to be followed to the end to win. The Greeks invented a feature that is still a common part of many board games today: the path with squares containing messages of reward or punishment coming to any player who lands there.

Persians enjoyed singing songs, storytelling, and reciting poetry. They played a variety of musical instruments, including harps, flutes, and tambourines.

GAMES AND FESTIVALS

The Greek tradition of elaborate, well-attended events moved east with Alexander. One of the most important ways the Greeks honored their gods was by holding various public festivals. In fact, the Greek calendar is filled with religious and civic contests and games. Athens had the largest number of religious festivals in Greece. Nearly half the days of the year featured a large or small festival.

Not everyone attended all the festivals. The contracts of hired laborers spelled out exactly which religious ceremonies they could attend. Married women had their own festival—a three-day celebration in honor of the goddess Demeter.

Some festivals honored gods with sacrifices and parades, and also with contests in music, dancing, poetry, and athletics. Valuable prizes were awarded to the winners. Funeral games honored a dead warrior by acting out his military skills. The most famous contests were the Olympic Games. These were open to all Greeks, and were held in the city of Olympia every four years during the summer.

Athletes in Alexander's time were all men. Slaves, foreigners, and convicts were barred from entering the games as competitors, Women were not allowed to watch the games at all. Winners were celebrated and received cash, free meals for the rest of their lives, did not have to pay taxes, and received other benefits.

Alexander and his men held festivals and tournaments wherever the army stopped for a time. For large festivals, they would create a city of tents for the actors, poets, singers, and musicians they brought from Greece. They set up banners on gilded poles, held gymnastic and literary competitions, and organized foot and chariot races.

EPILOGUE

FROM THE WESTERN EDGES OF THE ONCE-IMPRESSIVE Persian Empire to the remote reaches of India and Pakistan, traces of Alexander the Great are still easy to find. Travel away from the modern, urban centers or speak to people who have lived in the same area for centuries. His influence shows up in the language, art, and customs of many lands Alexander once claimed.

The name of Alexander is still spoken in countless tales, both heroic and horrifying. The far-reaching impact of Alexander's conquests still resounds today.

One of the most profound aspects of this impact was bringing the Greek language and customs into the areas under his dominion. By doing so, he set the stage for the rapid exchange of knowledge and ideas over thousands of miles and throughout many formerly unconnected cultural groups.

TALES OF TRIUMPH AND TERROR

Traces of Alexander are found in the names associated with the many places he claimed for himself and beyond. From the mountains of the Hindu Kush to the capital of Egypt to the eastern shores of the Mediterranean and even beyond, reminders of Alexander are found in preserved art and crumbling architecture. Old coins exchanged in rural markets seem straight out of the 2,000-year-old past. And of course, Alexander is the central figure in hundreds of stories.

Just inland from the eastern Mediterranean coast stand the massive ruins of Apollo's temple of Didyma. Alexander stopped there early in his

OPPOSITE

The fame of Alexander swept the ancient world and influenced people for centuries. Legends sprang up about him that are still told in far corners of the world today. This 1597 painting from India shows Alexander in a sea battle.

The Last Greek Inscription

In the 1930s, archaeologists excavated a huge tower close to Persepolis and facing the Naqsh-e Rustam tombs of the Achaemenian kings. On the tower were writings in Greek, Parthian, and Middle Persian. They described the successful wars against Rome waged by Persian king Shapur I (d. 272 C.E.) in the third century. Historians consider this a significant record because it was the last time the Greek language appeared in any Iranian inscription.

eastward campaign. Legend has it that the sacred spring there had dried up after the Persians looted and desecrated the temple in 494 B.C.E. But when Alexander arrived to honor to Apollo, they say, the spring suddenly began to flow again. Soon after, according to the ancient writings, the new priestess of the temple predicted King Darius's death and Alexander's triumph in the east.

The whole of Alexander's journey is marked with spots like this. The so-called Wall of Alexander is a fortress wall built at the northern edge of today's Iran by Parthian kings after Alexander's death. It stretches east from the Caspian Sea for 124 miles.

In Herat, Afghanistan, the rough-looking mud brick remains of an old fort mark the area where he founded his city of Alexandria in Areia. In Kandahar, Afghanistan, archaeologists discovered a temple portraying Alexander as a god, with inscriptions in Greek and the biblical language of Aramaic.

In 1939, a huge treasure was found north of Kabul, at the foot of the Hindu Kush Mountains where Alexander had a base. When the remains of this Hellenistic city were unearthed, archaeologists retrieved Greek glassware, and Greek style ivory sculptures from India and lacquered objects from China. All are evidence of the trade that began blossoming under Alexander's rule.

All this is just a small fraction of the physical evidence that remains in the 21st century, and on four continents, of a ruthlessly ambitious conqueror. But Alexander's life, and his powerful and contradictory personality, comes most alive in the hundreds of stories that have been preserved and passed down over the centuries.

In particular, the stories, plays, and songs that portray him at his most fearsome tell of the Great Iskander (Arabic for Alexander)—the destroying, two-horned beast.

The tales of Alexander's evil exploits are gleefully relayed in dusty roadside *caravanserai*, or inns. They are danced to by campfires in ancient mountains. Modern-day Middle Eastern children listened to them in their bedrooms at night. He even shows up in Muslim Shiite folk plays, where his clothing often includes jodhpurs (English-style riding pants) and a safari helmet.

The tales of Alexander's life and deeds range from reasonably believable to laughably impossible. They are not confined to the lands that he conquered, either. He stars in legends and romances originating in places

as far away as Western Europe, China, and Ethiopia. In some works, Alexander's father, King Philip, is portrayed as a Christian martyr and Alexander himself as a holy religious saint.

One common story told throughout Asia even today is also depicted on old sculptures in some European cathedrals. It tells of Alexander as the two-horned monster who takes over the entire world. Then, still full of ambition, he plans to ride a chariot into the heavens, like a god. His destruction comes when God throws him down for being consumed by pride.

In the telling of these tales over time, Alexander has taken on mythical proportions. Like any hero or monster worth remembering, he is

This fanciful scene of Alexander shows him being carried through the air by mythical griffins—creatures with the body of a lion and the head and wings of an eagle.

larger than life, coming through the centuries to us as fabulous, ferocious, and wondrous.

THE FATE OF MACEDON

Like Alexander himself, Macedon's story after the death of Alexander is neither simple nor peaceful. When Alexander's successor in Macedon, Cassander, grabbed the throne, it led to civil war. There was political unrest and a lack of clear leadership for nearly the next 50 years.

In 276 B.C.E., Antigonus II (320–239 B.C.E.) became king of Macedon. He finally brought some stability to the country and started a dynasty that lasted until 168 B.C.E.

During the second and third centuries B.C.E., Macedon went to war with Rome four times. The results were disastrous the last three times. At the end of the fourth war, which lasted from 149 to 148 B.C.E., Macedon was made a province of a Roman Empire that was just at the beginning of its rise to power.

Because of its unique geographical position as a crossroads between east and west, Macedon has historically been a desired possession for invaders coming from every direction. It was considered a crucial territory during the Byzantine Empire. Near the end of the 14th century it was absorbed into the large territory ruled by the Turkish Ottoman Empire. Macedon remained relatively stable under this influence until 1912, when the Turks were finally pushed out of Europe by an alliance among Greece, Serbia, Montenegro, and Bulgaria. This conflict became known as the first Balkan War.

More than 500 years of Islamic rule under the Ottomans had a huge effect on every aspect of Macedon's culture. Everything from religion to politics to daily customs of eating and dress were influenced by the Turks. The mix of different ethnic groups and cultural traditions further complicated the Macedonian national identity.

When the winners in the Balkan Wars divided up the lands they had taken from the Turks, the territory that Alexander the Great had once called home was split into three parts.

The southern portion, Greek Macedon, became a part of Greece. This is where the capital and the political center of the ancient kingdom of Macedon are located. It is still part of modern Greece. The northern portion of Macedon, except for a small territory given to Bulgaria, went to Serbia. This section became known as Macedonia.

Alexander Goes to Hollywood

Alexander has also made a name for himself in Hollywood. In 1955, actor Richard Burton starred in the film *Alexander the Great*. And in the fall of 2004, he was reincarnated again. This time audiences saw him (played by Colin Farrell) do heroic battle in the Oliver Stone movie *Alexander*.

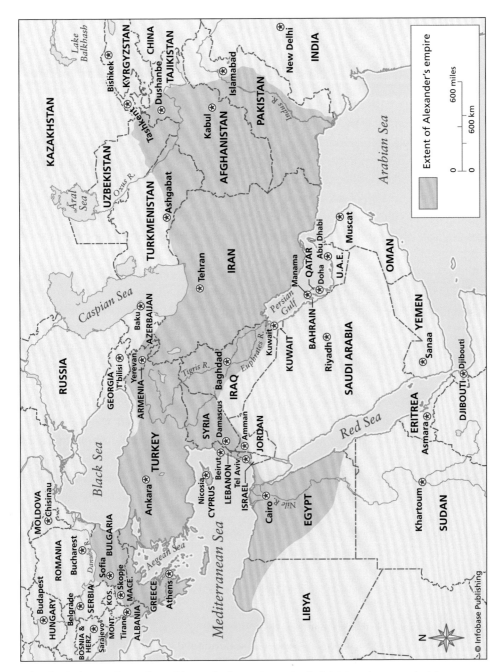

The shaded area shows how Alexander's empire at its height touches on what is now more than a dozen countries in Western Europe, the Middle East, and Asia.

MACEDONIA TODAY

After World War I, a new kingdom was formed made up of Serbian Macedonia, Croatia, and Slovenia. This became the country of Yugoslavia in 1929.

In the following years, this northern part of Macedonia was constantly subjected to manipulation by outsiders who were trying to impose their own various visions of what the country should be. Finally in 1991, as Yugoslavia was breaking apart, the country declared its independence as The Republic of Macedonia.

However, a large part of ancient Macedon is still in Greece. The complexities of this situation, and the difficulties that arise from the country's ethnic mix, continue to cause much confusion and international concern in the modern world.

Greece loudly objected to Macedonia's name. The Greeks believed that by calling itself Macedonia, the new republic was making an attempt to lay claim to ancient Macedonian land in Greece. Under this pressure from Greece, the new republic modified its name to the Former Yugoslav Republic of Macedonia in 1993, when it was admitted to the United Nations.

Beginning in 2004, the United States and other countries recognized it as the Republic of Macedonia. Greece, however, continues to object. Through the middle of 2008, the dispute continued. Both the European Union and NATO were threatening to keep Macedonia from joining those organizations if they could not agree with Greece on a lasting solution. Macedonia did agree to redesign its flag—which had featured the ancient Greek symbol known as the Star of Vergina.

These days, the people of the Republic of Macedonia are, for the most part, of Slavic descent. But for many, their connections to Greek culture still play a large part in their identity. This means they are not willing to give up claims to having roots in ancient Macedon where Alexander grew up and ruled.

The existence of two Macedonias, one north and independent and one south in Greece, poses huge questions. These questions—particularly those of what defines the true Macedonia, who Macedonia belongs to, and most significantly, who the "real" Macedonians are—have caused raging debate and political moves for decades. It does not look like a resolution is near at hand.

JUDGING ALEXANDER

Alexander the Great is a fascinating figure. Historians and scholars continue to write books and make movies about him. Each writer puts their own interpretation on their famous subject, making it difficult to know exactly who he really was. No documents from Alexander's time have survived; all existing accounts of his deeds were written after his death. Many accounts contain conflicting information, making it even more difficult to know the truth about many of the events of his life.

Many of those who have told Alexander's story have been biased. They have slanted or exaggerated the truth sometimes for and sometimes against him. The broader picture of his conquests and some of

---

IN THEIR OWN WORDS

"The Accursed Alexander"

Even today, the Zoroastrians tell stories about the terrible religious persecution of Alexander. They say he killed their priests and ordered the holy book of Zoroastrianism, the Avesta, to be destroyed. In fact, it is likely that many sacred texts were destroyed when the palace at Persepolis was burned.

This description is from the Book of Arda Wiraz, which dates from the third or fourth century C.E. It is a religious text that describes the dream-journey of a devout Zoroastrian through the next world. It is his vision of heaven and hell, and Alexander is definitely part of hell.

They say that, once upon a time, the pious Zarathustra made the religion, which he had received, current in the world; and till the completion of 300 years, the religion was in purity, and men were without doubts. But afterward, the accursed Evil Spirit, the Wicked One, in order to make men doubtful of this religion, instigated the

accursed Alexander, the westerner who was dwelling in Egypt, so that he came to the country of Iran with severe cruelty and war and devastation; he also slew the ruler of Iran, and destroyed the metropolis and empire, and made them desolate.

And this religion, namely, all the Avesta and Zand, written upon prepared cow-skins, and with gold ink, was deposited in the archives, in Ishtakr [Persepolis], and the hostility of the evil-destined, wicked Ashemok, the evil-doer, brought onward Alexander, the westerner, who was dwelling in Egypt, and he burned them up. And he killed several high priests and judges and priests and the masters of the Magians and upholders of the religion, and the competent and wise of the country of Iran. . . .

(Source: "Book of Arda Wiraz." Livius Articles on Ancient History. Available online. URL: http://www.livius.org/aj-al/alexander/alexander_t47.html. Accessed June 13, 2008.)

IN THEIR OWN WORDS

Napoleon on Alexander

French military and political leader Napoleon Bonaparte (1769–1821) wrote about past military leaders whom he admired. He called them the Great Captains of Antiquity, and they included Alexander, Hannibal, Caesar, Frederick the Great.

Alexander, when scarcely more than a small boy and with a mere handful of troops, conquered one fourth of the globe, but was this on his part a simple eruption or an unexpected deluge? No. Everything was profoundly calculated, executed with audacity, and conducted with wisdom. . . .

His war was methodical and is worthy of the greatest praise. None of his convoys was ever intercepted, his armies always progressed by growing stronger. They were weakest at Granicus, in the

beginning. On the Indus they had tripled, not counting the troops under the orders of the governors of conquered provinces. . . .

What I love about Alexander . . . is not the campaigns themselves . . . but his political means. He left behind, at age 33, an immense, well-established empire that the generals divided amongst themselves. He had the art of making conquered people love him. He showed himself to be at one and the same time a great warrior, politician, and lawgiver. Unfortunately, when he attained the zenith of his glory and success, either his head turned him or his heart was spoiled.

(Source: *Napoleon on the Art of War*. Jay Luvaas, editor and translator. New York: Simon and Schuster, 2001.)

the facts of his background and life have been confirmed by historians. But many more facts and details will never be known with any certainty.

Alexander the Great has been considered both a god and a saint. Some believed he had divine powers. Paintings have depicted him wearing a halo.

On the other hand, priests of the Zoroastrian faith, Persia's dominant religion before Alexander's conquests, demonized Alexander. Their legends paint him as one of the most evil people in history.

Arabs, who came to know him as Iskander, described him as a kind of bogeyman. The Greek city-states, his unwilling allies to whom he sent a fortune in war spoils, considered him a tyrant and rejoiced when he died.

Many critics have painted Alexander as an alcoholic. Supporters have defended his heavy drinking, saying this was the regular practice of his times.

Critics have pointed to the brutality of some of his battles and the cruel murder and enslavement of some of his victims, including women and children. Supporters point to the fact that he did not allow his soldiers to rape women in lands they conquered and that he often pardoned enemies who surrendered. Some historians salute him as an enlightened leader because he tried to unite all his subjects and to treat all races as equals. Others believe he abused his power, killing his detractors and demanding that people worship him.

One fact historians do not dispute is that Alexander was one of the greatest military commanders of all time. He never lost a major battle. Both Julius Caesar and Napoleon looked up to him as the ideal military leader.

The young Macedonian king was also a great explorer. In this role, he went all the way to the ends of what was considered the inhabited

Is this Alexander the Great? This carved head was discovered in 1995 in the Turkish city of Sagalassos, which Alexander conquered in 333 B.C.E.

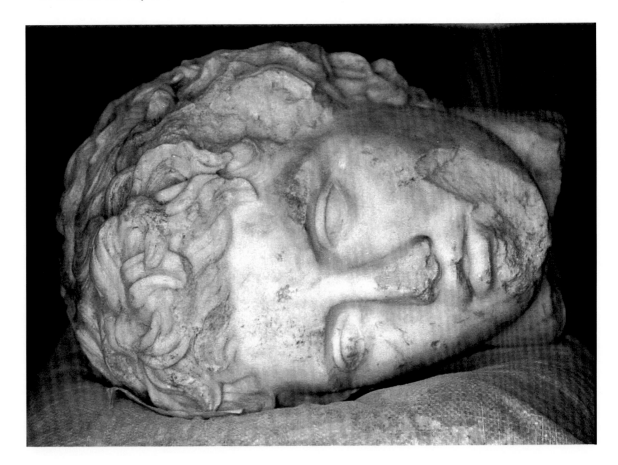

earth. He opened up both sea and land routes that connected separate parts of the world for the first time. It was not until the voyages of the Portuguese and Spanish in the late 15th century that Europeans finally explored farther than Alexander had.

In judging Alexander the conqueror, it is important to consider the historical and cultural context of his life. Although today we consider the invasion of another country to be a crime, the idea that waging war is morally evil was not introduced until the beginning of the 19th century. During Alexander's times, invading and taking over another country was not rare or even considered wrong. In fact, it was expected of a king.

As perhaps the most powerful leader of all antiquity, Alexander the Great more than fulfilled those expectations. Since the time of his own life, his contradictory personality—his extremes of valor, violence, and generosity—has held the attention of many. They try to understand the man behind the master military general. The glory and ferocity of his acts still echo down the centuries. Alexander the Great remains as fascinating in modern times as he was more than 2,000 years ago.

TIME LINE

356 B.C.E.	Alexander is born in Pella, Macedon.
338 B.C.E.	King Philip of Macedon conquers Athens and Thebes in the battle of Chaeronaea. Alexander commands the left flank of his father's army.
336 B.C.E.	King Philip is murdered. Alexander becomes king of Macedon.
335 B.C.E.	Alexander destroys the Greek city of Thebes as punishment for its revolt.
334 B.C.E.	Alexander invades Asia Minor. He defeats King Darius III of Persia at the Battle of the Granicus River.
333 B.C.E.	Alexander defeats Darius III at the Battle of Issus.
332 B.C.E.	Alexander conquers Tyre after a seven-month siege.
331 B.C.E.	Egypt surrenders to Alexander and crowns him pharaoh (king). Alexander establishes the city of Alexandria. Alexander defeats Darius III at the Battle of Gaugamela. Alexander is hailed as king of the Persian Empire.
330 B.C.E.	Darius III is murdered by his own military officers.
330–327 B.C.E.	Alexander conquers the eastern part of the Persian Empire.
327 B.C.E.	Alexander defeats the Sogdian leader, Oxyartes, and marries his daughter, Roxane.
326 B.C.E.	Alexander invades India. Alexander defeats King Porus at the Battle of Hydaspes. Alexander's troops refuse to continue, forcing him to return to Persia.
324 B.C.E.	Alexander organizes a mass marriage at Susa and marries his second and third wives. Alexander's closest friend, Hephaestion, dies in Persia.
323 B.C.E.	Alexander dies in Babylon on June 10, at the age of 32. A power struggle erupts for control of his kingdom. Alexander's son with his first wife, Roxane, is born shortly after his father's death. He is also named Alexander.
310 B.C.E.	Cassander, the new king of Macedon, executes Roxane and Alexander's son, who is 13 years old.
ca. 280 B.C.E.	The battles over Alexander's empire are finally settled. The empire is divided among Ptolemy in Egypt, Seleucus in Persia, and Antigonus in Greece and Macedon.
148 B.C.E.	Macedon becomes a province of the Roman Empire.
64 B.C.E.	The Seleucid dynasty in Persia ends when its western regions are taken over by the Roman Empire.
30 B.C.E.	The Ptolemaic dynasty ends in Egypt with the death of Queen Cleopatra VII. Egypt, too, becomes part of the Roman Empire.

GLOSSARY

agora an open-air marketplace

allies countries or groups that work together, especially during wartime; their unity is called an *alliance*

archaeologist a scientist who studies ancient peoples by studying the items they left behind

archer a person who shoots with a bow and arrow

architect a person who designs and builds buildings

aristocracy a small group of people of the highest class or who have the most money and power; individual members of this group are aristocrats

Asia Minor a broad peninsula that lies between the Black Sea and the Mediterranean Sea and corresponds roughly to modern Turkey

barbarians people considered to be uncivilized and uncultured

battering ram a heavy object swung or rammed against a door or wall to break it down

caravan a group of people traveling together, often traders

catapult a military machine used for hurling large objects

cavalry soldiers who fight on horseback

chariot a light, fast cart pulled by horses

city-state a city and its surrounding farms that functions as a separate nation

commerce the activity of buying and selling

divination the practice of seeking to know the future

dynasty a family that keeps control of a government over many generations, with rule often passed from a parent to a child

fertile the ability to easily grow (for plants) or have offspring (for animals and people)

flank the side of a large group of people, such as an army

garrison a fortified town where soldiers live

Hellas the word the Greeks used to mean the entire Greek world; what Greeks today call their nation

Hellenism Greek culture; the adjective is *Hellenistic*

hoplite a heavily armed Greek foot soldier

infantry soldiers who fight on foot

javelin a light spear that is thrown

logic the study of the rules and tests of sound reasoning

mercenary a foreign soldier hired to fight for another country

monarchy a government controlled by a king

omen a sign that predicts the future

oracle a priest or priestess who is said to be able to communicate with the gods and deliver messages from them

peninsula an area of land surrounded by water on three sides

phalanx a group of soldiers standing and moving in very close formation

philosopher a person who thinks about the meaning of life and how to lead a better life; in ancient times, many philosophers were also scientists

philosophy the study of the nature of the world

polygamy   having more than one wife at the same time

rhetoric   the art of speaking or writing effectively

sarissa   a long wooden spear with an iron tip

satrap   a regional governor in Persia

siege   cutting off a town or fort from the outside so it cannot receive supplies and the inhabitants cannot escape

siege engine   a machine that throws a projectile

soothsayer   a person who tells what will happen in the future, based on signs

successor   a person who comes after another and inherits or continues in the offices they held

tactic   an action or strategy that is carefully planned to achieve a specific result

trireme   a long, narrow Athenian warship powered by three rows of oarsmen

tyrant   a person who uses their power in a cruel and unreasonable way

BIBLIOGRAPHY

"Alexander the Great." Encarta Online Encyclopedia. Available online. URL: http://encarta.msn.com/encyclopedia_761564408/Alexander_the_Great.html. Accessed May 20, 2004.

"Alexander the Great." Classic Encyclopedia. Available online. URL: http://www.1911encyclopedia.org/ ALEXANDER_THE_GREAT. Accessed May 20, 2004.

"Antiqua Medicina From Homer to Vesalius." University of Virginia Medical School. Available online. URL: http://www.healthsystem.virginia.edu/internet/library/wdc-lib/historical/artifacts/antiqua/. Accessed June 13, 2008.

Arrian, *The Campaigns of Alexander.* Translated by Aubrey de Sélincourt. New York: Viking Penguin, 1982.

——, "The Speech of Alexander the Great." Ancient History Sourcebook. Available online. URL: http://www.fordham.edu/HALSALL/ancient/arrian-alexander1.htm. Accessed June 1, 2008.

"Battleship." Encyclopædia Britannica Online. Available online. URL: http://search.eb.com/eb/article?eu=13962. Accessed May 15, 2004.

The Bible, authorized King James version. Oxford, U.K.: Oxford University Press, 1992.

Bienkowski, Piotr, and Millard, Alan, *Dictionary of the Ancient Near East.* Philadelphia: University of Pennsylvania Press, 2000.

"Book of Arda Wiraz." Livius Articles on Ancient History. Available online. URL: http://www.livius.org/aj-al/alexander/alexander_t47.html. Accessed June 13, 2008.

Borza, Eugene N., editor, *The Impact of Alexander the Great.* Hinsdale, Ill.: The Dryden Press, 1974.

Carassava, Anthee, "NATO Could Block Macedonia Over Name." The New York Times Online, March 4, 2008. Available online. URL: http://www.nytimes.com/2008/03/04/world/europe/04nato.html?_r=2&oref=slogin&oref=slogin. Accessed June 20, 2008.

Cotterell, Arthur, editor, *The Penguin Encyclopedia of Classical Civilizations.* Middlesex, U.K.: The Penguin Group, 1993.

Cowan, Ross, *Roman Legionary, 58 B.C.–A.D. 69.* Oxford and London, U.K.: Osprey Publishing, 2003.

Curtius Rufus, Quintus. *History of Alexander the Great of Macedonia.* Translated by John Yardley. "Alexander Takes Tyre." URL: http://www.livius.org/aj-al/alexander/alexander_t09.html. Accessed June 10, 2008.

——, *History of Alexander the Great of Macedonia.* Translated by John Yardley. "Alexander in the Bactrian Desert." Available online. URL: http://www.livius.org/aj-al/alexander/alexander_t17.html. Accessed June 10, 2008.

"Dreadnought." Encyclopædia Britannica Online. Available online. URL: http://search.eb.com/eb/article?eu=31678. Accessed May 5, 2004.

Fox, Robin Lane, *Alexander the Great.* London: Penguin Books, 1973.

"Greece." Livius Articles on Ancient History. Available online. URL: http://www.livius.org/greece.html. Accessed May 28, 2004.

Hart-Davis, Adam, "Discovering Roman Technology." BBC Ancient History—Romans. Available online. URL: http://www.bbc.co.uk/history/ancient/romans/tech_01.shtml. Accessed June 1, 2008.

Hayes, Carlton J. H., *Ancient Civilizations: Prehistory to the Fall of Rome.* New York: MacMillan Publishing Co., 1983.

Herodotus, *The Histories.* Translated by Aubrey de Sélincourt. New York: Penguin Classics, 1972.

Lahanas, Michael, "Ancient Greek Artillery from Catapults to the Architronio Canon." Available online. URL: http://www.mlahanas.de/Greeks/war/CatapultTypes.htm. Accessed June 28, 2004.

Luvaas, Jay, editor and translator, *Napoleon on the Art of War.* New York: Simon and Schuster, 2001.

"Macedonia." Encyclopædia Britannica Online. Available online. URLs: http://search.eb.com/ebi/article?eu=297567; http://search.eb.com/ebi/article?eu=297568; http://search.eb.com/eb/article?eu=119675;http://search.eb.com/eb/article?eu=119677; http://search.eb.com/eb/article?eu=50900; http://search.eb.com/eb/article?eu=50901; http://search.eb.com/eb/article?eu=50902. Accessed May 10, 2004.

Meyers, Eric M., editor, *The Oxford Encyclopedia of Archeology in the Near East.* New York: Oxford University Press, 1997.

"A Monumental Building in a City of Magnificent Intentions." Office of the Curator, Department of the Treasury Exhibition—Greek Revival Architecture in Washington, D.C. Available online. URL: http://www.ustreas.gov/offices/management/curator/exhibitions/2002exhibit/greekrevival.html. Accessed May 2, 2004.

"Naval Ship." Encyclopædia Britannica Online. Available online. URL: http://search.eb.com/eb/article?eu=118842; http://search.eb.com/eb/article?eu=118843. Accessed May 2, 2004.

"Pasni, Pakistan: 25°17'17.23"N 63°20'37.76"E." Global Security. Available online. URL: http://www.globalsecurity.org/military/facility/pasni.htm. Accessed April 10, 2004.

Plutarch, *The Age of Alexander: Nine Greek Lives.* Translated by Ian Scott-Kilvert. New York: Penguin Classics, 1973.

——, *Alexander.* Translated by John Dryden. "The Internet Classics Archive." URL: http://classics.mit.edu/Plutarch/alexandr.html. Accessed June 10, 2008.

——, *Greek Lives.* Translated by Robin Waterfield. New York: Oxford University Press, 1999.

Pseudo-Callisthenes, *The Greek Alexander Romance.* Translated by Richard Stoneman. New York. Penguin, 1991.

Rahnamoon, Fariborz, "History of Persian or Parsi Language." Iran Chamber Society. Available online. URL: http://www.iranchamber.com/literature/articles/persian_parsi_language_history.php. Accessed March 17, 2004.

Ramet, Ph.D., Sabrina P., "Macedonia." Chicago: World Book Encyclopedia Interactive CD, 2004 edition.

Renault, Mary, *The Nature of Alexander.* New York: Pantheon Books, 1975.

Sadek, Samir, "The Mouseion Revisited." Al-Ahram Weekly Online (No. 668), December 11–17, 2003. Available online. URL: http://weekly.ahram.org.eg/2003/668/he1.htm. Accessed March 12, 2004.

Sekunda, Nick, *Republican Roman Army, 200–104 B.C.* Oxford and London, U.K.: Osprey Publishing, 1999.

"Spices: Exotic Flavors and Medicines." UCLA History and Special Collections, Louise M. Darling Biomedical Library. Available online. URL: http://unitproj.library.ucla.edu/biomed/spice/. Accessed July 7, 2004.

Vlamis, Christos Thomas, editor, "Arachaeonia: A Journey Through Ancient Greece." Available online. URL: http://archaeonia.com. Accessed June 4, 2004.

Wallace, Daniel B., *Greek Grammar Beyond the Basics.* Grand Rapids, Mich.: Zondervan, 1996.

Welles, C. Bradford, *Alexander and the Hellenistic World.* Toronto, Ontario.: A.M. Hakkert, Ltd., 1970.

Welman, Nick, "All About Alexander the Great." Pothos.org. Available online. URL: http://www.pothos.org/content/. Accessed July 23, 2004.

Whitehouse, David, "Library of Alexandria Discovered." BBC News, UK Edition Online, May 12, 2004. Available online. URL: http://news.bbc.co.uk/1/hi/sci/tech/3707641.stm. Accessed June 13, 2008.

Wood, Michael, *In the Footsteps of Alexander the Great: A Journey from Greece to Asia.* Berkeley and Los Angeles, Calif.: University of California Press, 1997.

Worthington, Ian, editor, *Alexander the Great: A Reader.* London and New York: Routledge, 2003.

"Yasna (sacred liturgy) Avesta." Zoroastrian Archives. Available online. URL: http://www.avesta.org/yasna/y0to8s.htm. Accessed May 5, 2008.

FURTHER RESOURCES

BOOKS

Behnke, Alison, *The Conquests of Alexander the Great* (Minneapolis, Minn.: Lerner Publishing Group, September 2007)

This very thorough book chronicles Alexander's successes and failures as a commander. The many battles and sieges are described in great detail, as are the various enemies that Alexander's army faced. His strength as a strategist in battle as well as his ability to absorb new cultures into his growing empire are discussed. There are maps of his route through the Middle East and Asia and interesting sidebars and illustrations of Alexander and his comrades. Detailed source notes, a thorough timeline, a who's who of the major players, and an explanation of the differences between primary and secondary sources are all provided.

Chrisp, Peter, *Alexander the Great: The Legend of a Warrior King* (New York: DK Publishing, 2003)

This book follows the history of Alexander the Great and his campaign to conquer the known world. It includes information on his traveling companions, armies of his time, ships, and food. There are a lot of illustrations and factoids.

Fildes, Alan, and Joann Fletcher, *Alexander the Great: Son of the Gods* (Los Angeles: Getty Publications, 2004)

This book offers a year-by-year account of Alexander's life. Among the topics covered are Alexander's family life, including the influence of his mother, Queen Olympias, his brilliant leadership, his devoted troops, and his daily life on the march and off duty. Many illustra-

tions, featuring ancient art from museums around the world, accompany the text.

Gergel, Tania, editor, *Alexander the Great: The Brief Life and Towering Exploits of History's Greatest Conqueror—As Told by His Original Biographers* (New York: Penguin, 2004)

This book knits together the accounts of several ancient historians to paint a picture of Alexander's life as it was understood in the few hundred years after he died. It includes selections from the writings of Greek historians Arrian and Plutarch, and Roman historian Quintus Curtius Rufus.

Greenblatt, Miriam, *Alexander the Great and Ancient Greece* (Tarrytown, N.Y.: Benchmark Books, 2000)

This short book is divided into two main sections. The first provides a brief history of Alexander and his conquests. The second describes everyday life in ancient Greece, including occupations, home, family life, clothing, religion, and customs. The book places Alexander in the context of his history and culture.

Gunther John, *Alexander the Great* (New York: Sterling Publishing Co., 2007)

Modern historian John Gunther tells the story of Alexander the Great. Gunther takes his readers from Alexander's boyhood to his victory over the Persian Empire. He describes Alexander's battles, as well as the palace intrigues that surrounded him.

Nardo, Don, *Philip II and Alexander the Great Unify Greece in World History* (Berkeley Heights, N.J.: Enslow Publishers, 2000)

This book is mostly about King Philip II of Macedon's success in unifying the Greek city-states in the fourth century B.C.E. But it also covers his son Alexander's rise to power after Philip's assassination. The portrayals of both men show their strengths and weaknesses. The author uses both primary and secondary sources to enrich the narrative.

DVDS

In the Footsteps of Alexander the Great (PBS Home Video, 2004)

This is the 1998 Public Television documentary with British filmmaker Michael Wood. Wood travels 20,000 miles, tracing the expedition of Alexander the Great. Relying on the words of Greek and Roman historians, Wood tries to follow Alexander's route as closely as possible. As he travels he explains what happened in each place where Alexander stopped. He also learns how much influence Alexander's presence continues to have. The journey begins in Greece and goes through 16 countries, including Turkey, Israel, Egypt, Iran, Afghanistan, and India. In the course of his travels, Wood passes through four war zones and he notes that strategic regions of Alexander's day are still important today.

The True Story of Alexander the Great (A&E Home Video, 2005)

This History Channel production is hosted by Peter Woodward. The documentary incorporates dramatic reenactments with state-of-the-art computer animation. Drawing on the expertise of renowned scholars, the documentary examines the life and career of this military genius and fearless leader.

WEB SITES

Achaemenid Persia
http://members.ozemail.com.au/~ancientpersia/index.html

This site contains information about ancient Persia during the Achaemenid dynasty—the dynasty that was eventually conquered by Alex-

ander the Great. The site has articles about history and time lines, and also takes a detailed look at Persian culture and everyday life. Fun pages include trivia, quizzes, and games.

Alexander the Great
www.fsmitha.com/h1/ch11.htm

This Web site provides a narrative history from historian Frank E. Smitha of Antiquity Online. Maps and links to other Alexander the Great sites are included. Opinions are clearly labeled as such. The site is especially useful for following what happened to Alexander's empire after his death. It moves forward all the way to the Roman Empire.

Alexander the Great
www.livius.org/aj-al/alexander/alexander00.html

This site includes 18 in-depth articles covering the life of Alexander chronologically. Each article has links to deeper levels of details, and there is a large index. The site explores history from both the Greek and Persian perspectives, drawing on 70 ancient sources. It was developed by educator Jona Lendering from Amsterdam. There are also photographs showing all the places Alexander went.

Alexander the Great on the Web
www.isidore-of-seville.com/Alexanderama.html

This site, edited by Tim Spaulding, is a Web directory of information about Alexander the Great. It provides exhaustive lists of and links to biographies, articles, papers, books, movies, television programs, maps, images of Alexander (and people dressing up as Alexander), and more. There are notes and short reviews about each resource. This site leads to hundreds of other links about every part of Alexander's life and legacy.

All About Alexander the Great
www.pothos.org

This comprehensive Web site was created by Thomas William-Powlett, a former educator. Other authors contribute articles to the site, which is maintained by a team of volunteers. It contains a general introduction to Alexander, book reviews, many articles divided by subject (from animals to battles), time lines, and a trivia quiz. A Travel Guide section looks at how the places Alexander visited and founded have changed through the ages, all the way to the present day.

The Army of Alexander the Great

http://members.tripod.com/~S_van_Dorst/ Alexander.html#macarmy

This site looks in detail at the Macedonian army. It breaks the subject down into cavalry, infantry, command structure, and other types of Greek forces in Alexander's army. There are also links to information about the ancient Greek army (including Greek military terms) and the ancient Roman army.

Hellenistic Greece

www.historyforkids.org/learn/greeks/history/ hellenistic.htm

This site is part of History for Kids. There is a short article about Alexander's life, with links to many aspects of his story—including Greek history and culture, sculpture, architecture, medicine, Alexander in India, ancient Persia, and how the Romans spread Hellenistic culture.

Picture Credits

INDEX

Note: **Boldface** page numbers indicate major discussions of topics; *italic* page numbers indicate illustrations; page numbers followed by *c* indicate chronology entries; page numbers followed by *g* indicate glossary entries; page numbers followed by *m* indicate maps.

ABOUT THE AUTHOR

DEBRA SKELTON began her writing career as a broadcast journalist. Her writing has appeared extensively in books, magazines, and a variety of educational media.

PAMELA DELL is the author of more than 40 books for children, including biographies, historical fiction, and science and social studies topics. She has written educational materials for, among others, *Encyclopaedia Britannica* and World Book, Inc., and is the creator and author of award-winning children's entertainment software titles.

History consultant **JOHN W. I. LEE** is associate professor of history at the University of California at Santa Barbara, specializing in the study of ancient Greece, Greek archaeology, and ancient warfare.